SERIES  TEACHING FILM AND MED

# Teaching
# Women and Film

## Sarah Gilligan

Series Editor: Vivienne Clark
Commissioning Editor: Wendy Earle

 Education

British Library Cataloguing-in-Publication Data
A catalogue record for this book is available from the British Library

**ISBN 0 85170 977 X**

First published in 2003 by the British Film Institute
21 Stephen Street, London W1T 1LN

Copyright © British Film Institute 2003
The copyright of this teaching guide belongs to the British Film Institute.

Student worksheets to support this guide are supplied at: www.bfi.org.uk/tfms
User name: **women**   Password: **te2 106wo**

Design: Amanda Hawkes
Cover photographs: *Elizabeth*, courtesy of *bfi* Stills
Printed in Great Britain by Cromwell Press

**www.bfi.org.uk**

The British Film Institute offers you opportunities to experience, enjoy and discover
more about the world of film and television.

# Contents

# Introduction to the series

The recent and rapid growth of both Film and Media Studies post-16 has inevitably led to a demand for more teachers for these popular courses. But, given the comparatively recent appearance of both subjects at degree level (and the limited availability of relevant post-graduate teaching courses), many new and experienced teachers from other disciplines are faced with teaching either subject for the first time, without a degree-level background.

In addition, the new post-16 specifications saw the arrival of new set topics and areas of study, and some of the specifications have changing topics, so there is a pressing need for up-to-date resources to help teacher preparation.

This new series has been developed with these factors – and the busy teacher – in mind. Each title aims to provide teachers with an accessible reference resource, with essential topic content, as well as clear guidance on good classroom practice to improve the quality of their teaching and learning. Every author in the series is an experienced practitioner of Film and/or Media Studies at this level, and many have examining/moderating experience.

## Key features:

- Assessment contexts
- Suggested schemes of work
- Historical contexts (where appropriate)
- Key facts, statistics and terms
- Detailed reference to the key concepts of Film and Media Studies
- Detailed case studies
- Glossaries
- Bibliographies
- Student worksheets, activities and resources (available online) – ready for you to print and photocopy for the classroom.

**Other titles in the series include**:
Teaching Scriptwriting, Screenplays and Storyboards for Film and TV Production; Teaching TV Sitcom; Teaching TV News; Teaching Film Language; Teaching TV Soaps; Teaching Video Games; Teaching World Cinema; Teaching British Broadcasting since 1990; Teaching British Cinema since 1990; Teaching Film Censorship and Controversy; Teaching Television Language; Teaching Music Videos.

**SERIES EDITOR: Vivienne Clark** is a former Head of Film and Media Studies. She is an Advanced Skills Teacher, an Associate Tutor of the British Film Institute and Principal Examiner for A Level Media Studies for one of the English awarding bodies. She is a freelance teacher trainer and writer/editor on Film and Media Studies, with several published textbooks and teaching resources. She is also a course tutor on the bfi/Middlesex University MA level module: An Introduction to Media Education (distance learning).

**Author: Sarah Gilligan** is Lecturer-in-Charge of Media at Hartlepool College of Further Education, where she currently runs courses on Media Studies and Media: Communication and Production. She has a range of experience in teaching Film, Media and Cultural Studies courses for various examining boards. In addition she is currently working on a PhD at Royal Holloway, University of London, on 'Clothing, Identity and Contemporary Cinema'.

# Introduction

## Assessment contexts

| Awarding body & level | Subject | Unit code | Module/Topic |
|---|---|---|---|
| ✓ OCR | Media Studies | 2732 | Case Study: Audiences and Institutions |
| ✓ AQA AS Level | Media Studies | MED1 | Reading Media Texts |
| ✓ AQA AS Level | Media Studies | MED2 | Textual Topics in Contemporary Media |
| ✓ AQA A2 Level | Media Studies | MED4 | Texts and Contexts in the Media |
| ✓ AQA A2 Level | Media Studies | MED6 | Comparative Critical Analysis |
| ✓ EdExcel AVCE | Media | Unit 1 | Analyse Media Products |
| ✓ EdExcel AVCE | Media | Unit 6 | Media Industries |
| ✓ OCR AS Level | Media Studies | 2731 | Textual Analysis |
| ✓ OCR A2 Level | Media Studies | 2734 | Critical Research Study |
| ✓ WJEC AS Level | Film Studies | FS1 | Film: Making Meaning 1 |
| ✓ WJEC AS Level | Film Studies | FS2 | Producers and Audiences: Hollywood and British Cinema |
| ✓ WJEC AS Level | Film Studies | FS3 | Messages and Values: British and Irish Cinema |
| ✓ WJEC A2 Level | Film Studies | FS4 | Film: Making Meaning 2 |
| ✓ WJEC A2 Level | Film Studies | FS6 | Critical Studies |
| ✓ SQA Higher | Media Studies | D332 | 12 Media Analysis |
| ✓ SQA Advanced Higher | Media Studies | D332 | 13 Media Analysis |
| ✓ SQA Advanced Higher | Media Studies | D37A | 13 Media Investigation |

## ● Specification links

The following specification links are possible through the study of women and film as a broad and a specialist topic:

## ● AQA AS/A2 Media Studies

### MED 4: Texts and Contexts. Studies in Depth
- Genre: Post-heritage
- Representation: Women, stars, male as object of the gaze

### MED1: Reading Media Texts and MED 6: Comparative Critical Analysis
- Develop skills in analysing film, television and print texts through applying the key concepts

### MED2: Textual Topics in Contemporary Media
- Film and broadcast fiction – textual analysis of film texts, especially in terms of narrative and the ways in which texts reach and appeal to different audiences
- Advertising and marketing – analysis of the persuasive techniques that are used in order to promote films to different segments of the audience

## ● EdExcel AVCE Media: Communication and Production (Single and Double Awards)

### Unit 1: Analyse Media Products
- Analysis of the front cover of magazines, advertisements – analysis of representation issues and narrative structures and techniques

### Unit 6: Media Industries
- Role of women in the industry

## ● OCR AS/A2 Media Studies

### 2734: Critical Research Study
- Set topic: Women and Film

### 2731: Textual Analysis
- Analysis of language and conventions in the study of specific texts, and possible linking to consumerism and lifestyle magazines, celebrity and the tabloid process, through a study of stars, consumption and audiences

- **WJEC AS/A2 Film Studies**

*FS1: Film: Making Meaning 1*
- Textual analysis, especially the use of costume

*FS2: Producers and Audiences: Hollywood and British Cinema*
- Stars and consumption

*FS3: Messages and Values: British and Irish Cinema*
- Developments in Post-heritage cinema

*FS4: Film: Making Meaning 2*
- Auteur research project (eg Gwyneth Paltrow, Kathryn Bigelow, Jane Campion)

*FS6: Critical Studies*
- Feminist perspectives
- Sociological perspectives
- Studies in performance
- Studies in genre and authorship

*Key Skills*
Links to key skills coverage – Communication and potentially AON and IT – through research, collating and analysing data, and for coursework projects.

- **SQA Higher/Advanced Higher Media Studies**

*D332 12 Media Analysis*
- Analysis of a range of texts: cinema, print, advertising, TV

*D332 13 Media Analysis*
- Application of Media and Film theory and debates to the analysis of a range of texts drawn from: cinema, print, advertising, TV.

*D37A 13 Media Investigation*
- Employment in the Film/Media industries
- Audiences and consumption
- Gender representation in media texts

# How to use this guide

This guide provides an introduction to methods and case studies to support the teaching of women and film to Media and Film Studies students at a range of levels. Its key aims are:

- To provide frameworks for studying women and film, in terms of women's involvement in the production of films, the representation of women in film and the processes of reception;
- To encourage students to develop an understanding of how feminist film theory can be integrated into the study and analysis of representation and genre;
- To encourage an intertextual approach to the study of film, in which students can draw upon a diverse range of evidence, drawn from close textual analysis.

While some key debates in feminist film theory are introduced, the intention of this guide is to make the theory and texts relevant and accessible to students and teachers and lecturers. The guide uses contemporary, mainstream examples wherever possible. Where older examples are used, they function to provide a historical context to underpin comparative critical analysis of the developments and changes in genre and representation. I have tried to use examples that are familiar to the students and to encourage you to draw upon not only texts that you enjoy, but also texts that the students themselves consume. The intention is that the approaches, concepts and examples within this guide act as a springboard to studying women and film. The case studies should ideally become the basis for comparative critical analysis, in which you and your students analyse the similarities, differences and developments between the case studies in this pack and other examples.

The study of women and film, relating to both the production and the reception of film, should ideally be integral to the study of film and media, and not be treated as a 'token' topic. There is a danger that, by separating women and film as a distinct topic, it becomes categorised as somehow 'other', different to the 'norm'. Therefore the purpose of this guide is to support the teaching of women and film both as a specialist topic and as an integral part of your teaching of topics and concepts such as, media industries, stars, audiences, representation and genre.

The guide begins with background information to the industrial and theoretical approaches to women and film. A timeline identifies key moments and texts, and there is an overview of the rise of feminist film theory, countercinema and issues of consumption and pleasure. The intention is that you should use such background information as a starting point – a base upon which to build. You should then focus upon contemporary case studies, rather than 'bolting on' chunks of theory; you should not ask students to discuss texts that they have not seen and/or find inaccessible.

Finally, the three case studies provide a framework for studying women and film:

- Women working in the film industry;
- Stars, representation and audiences, focusing on Gwyneth Paltrow;

● Genre, representation and media language, focusing on Heritage and Post-heritage film and costume analysis.

These case studies encourage an intertextual approach, through the research and analysis of television, advertising and marketing, magazines, press, and websites.

The guide is supported by a variety of online resources that provide further information and case studies, together with worksheets that encourage students to reflect upon their own consumption of film, develop skills in textual analysis and undertake independent research. The worksheets to support these exercises are available at www.bfi.org.uk/tfms. To access the pages, enter username: **women** and the password: **te2106wo**. If you have any problems, email: education.resources@bfi.org.uk.

These pages also supply further information on approaching women and film. See the supplementary teaching notes at www.bfi.org.uk/tfms: Ten top tips for making women and film and feminist film theory accessible.

# Schemes of work

## ● Scheme of work 1: Industry – audience – genre

This unit has been designed as a six-week block to briefly introduce key issues of industry, audience and genre. In this form it would work best with AS Level students as a means of introducing key ideas/debates about pleasure, consumption, genre and institution that should underpin their understanding throughout the course.

If undertaken in the later months of the AS year, the unit enables the introduction of debates and analysis that can be used for case studies of film and broadcast fiction. It also introduces work that could be developed in much further depth in A2, as coursework and/or in-depth genre case studies (eg for AQA MED4: Texts and Contexts). In addition to working as a genre case study (changes over time, playful and ironic use of genre, multi-generic hybrids etc), debates in Heritage/Post-heritage cinema can be used to explore the advertising and marketing of films, together with the representation of gender, sexuality and national identity.

Aims:    To promote understanding of
1. The gender divide in employment in the film industry;
2. Issues of pleasure and consumption by audiences of the media – especially film;
3. The historical development of genre.

Outcomes:

- Compilation and analysis of data relating to women working in the film industry;
- Comparative critical analysis of a range of texts and trailers.

**Week 1**  Introduction to industry

Creating a voice for women – feminist and independent film production and feminist theory/politics

Women currently working in the film industry in front and behind the camera

The gender divide – female stars and male creators

Overview of findings from Martha M Lauzen's study *The Celluloid Ceiling: Behind-the-Scenes Employment of Women in the Top 250 Films of 2001*

(**Worksheet 2**)

**Week 2**  Case studies on women currently working behind the camera

Students to compile, collate, present and analyse data on women working behind the camera on recent mainstream releases (either currently at the cinema and/or Oscar-nominated and/or box-office hits of the past year)

Possible integrated key skills assignment: Communication, ICT and AON. Research using a range of sources (including ICT), present data as a report – supported by illustrations, numerical data and tables/graphs, and presentation to an audience and discussion (**Worksheet 7**)

**Week 3**  Audiences, pleasure and consumption

Negotiated and guilty pleasures – including patterns/modes of consumption and the pleasures of magazines

Female- versus male-centred narratives

*Sex and the City* (any episode – make sure though that you assess its suitability in terms of content for use with your students, to save embarrassment!) – constructing a mainstream female-centred narrative. What pleasures are offered by the text?

Representation of gender and sexuality. Where does *Sex and the City* place the male spectator? See www.bfi.org.uk/tfms for a *Sex and the City* case study

(**Worksheets 5** and **6**)

**Week 4**  Genre case study

Defining genre

Conventions of Heritage cinema and existing academic debates

Analysis of the trailer for A *Room with a View*

Re-reading the Heritage film – costume and landscape, and the pleasures of the male

See www.bfi.org.uk/tfms for handout on the characteristics of Heritage films

(**Worksheets 25** and **26**)

**Week 5**  Changes in the Heritage film

Moving into the mainstream: Jane Campion's *The Piano*

Conventions of Post-heritage cinema

Analysis of the advertising and marketing of *Shakespeare in Love* and *Elizabeth*. Tie-in with the role of the Oscars to promote films

How are the more recent films self-consciously similar/different to Heritage? How do they use elements of multiple genres and stars in order to appeal to a wider audience?

See www.bfi.org.uk/tfms for a handout on the characteristics of the post-*Piano* film

**Week 6**  Recent changes in the Post-heritage film

Analysis of recent films which are mainstream, playful, ironic, multi-generic and male-centred narratives:

*Moulin Rouge!*
*Plunkett and Macleane*
*Gangs of New York*

Essay: Genre – changes over time and/or pleasure and genre and/or use of conventions of more than one genre

## ● Scheme of work 2: Representation

This unit has been designed as a six-week block to introduce issues of representation with a focus upon gender and sexuality. This unit would work best with A2 students, as it enables you to develop student's synoptic knowledge and skills in comparative critical analysis.

While gender and sexuality are the main focus within this unit, there is the potential to analyse the texts in terms of issues of race and national identity. Be wary, though. Try not to analyse 'everything' because cramming too much in means that students lose sight of the central issues and debates, and you also run the risk of never getting beyond analysing the first scene.

Within this unit, students will be encouraged to analyse the intertextuality of the image of the star in creating points of identification, aspiration and desire. In addition, the ways in which costume can be seen not only to support character construction, but also to act as a means of constructing gendered identity are explored.

The scheme of work refers to a number of worksheets that are available in the online resource collection for this pack.

Aims    To promote understanding of
- The processes of representation in the media – especially through film;
- The construction and performance of gendered and sexual identity;
- The relationship between stars, identification and consumption.

Outcomes:
- Comparative analysis of representation in films from a range of genres;
- Critical analysis of the intertextual use of stars.

**Week 1**   Introduction to stars

What is a star, what do they do? (**Worksheet 13**)

Key points to remember about stars

Typecasting and cultural myths (**Worksheets 3**, **12**, **18**)

The pleasures of stars – introduction/overview of Jackie Stacey's *Star Gazing: Hollywood Cinema and Female Spectatorship* (**Worksheets 16** and **20**)

**Week 2**   Intertextual representations of the star

Which stars are we encouraged to copy? Could extend to celebrities – eg the Beckhams

Identification, fragmentation, trademarks and consumption

Stars and brand endorsement

The Oscars and fashion

**(Worksheets 17, 23, 24)**

**Week 3**  Representations of a star

Focus on a current release, featured in a number of magazine/ newspaper articles

Comparative analysis of front covers – women's/men's magazines featuring the same star – and ways in which the star is represented to appeal to different audiences

Comparative analysis of the representation of Gwyneth Paltrow in *A Perfect Murder* and *Sliding Doors*:

Representations of femininity and heterosexual relationships

Tales of transformation

**(Worksheets 21, 22)**

Possible further analysis of Paltrow in *The Royal Tenenbaums*, *Shallow Hal*

**Week 4**  Gender and costume analysis

Analysis of costume in *Elizabeth*

The transformation of identity

Issues of sexuality/virginity

Icons and power

**(Worksheet 27)**

**Week 5**  Gender, sexuality and costume analysis

Gender performance, subversion, slippage and desire in *Shakespeare in Love*

**(Worksheets 28, 29, 30, 31)**

**Week 6**  Representations of masculinity and homoerotic desire

Comparative analysis:

Male as feminised object of the gaze in *A Room with a View*, *Elizabeth*, *Shakespeare in Love*

Homoerotic desire in the action genre – analysis of *Point Break*

**(Worksheet 8)**

# Background information

## Women and film timeline

A summary of key individuals and events in the film industry and in the development of film theory.

2003　The professional association Women in Film and Television (WFTV) launches the initiative Directing Change.

Colleen Atwood wins the Oscar for Best Achievement in Costume Design for *Chicago* (2002, Marty Richards)

2002　Halle Berry becomes the first black woman to win an Oscar for Best Actress in a Leading Role for *Monster's Ball* (2001, Marc Forster).

*Moulin Rouge!* (2001, Baz Luhrmann) wins two Oscars: Best Art Direction/Set Decoration (Catherine Martin – Art Director, Brigitte Broch – Set Decorator), and Best Costume Design (including Catherine Martin) and is nominated for a further six, including Best Editing (Jill Bilcock).

1999　*Shakespeare in Love* (1998, John Madden) wins seven Oscars (and is nominated for a further six) including: Best Actress in Leading Role (Gwyneth Paltrow), Best Actress in a Supporting Role (Judi Dench), Best Costume Design (Sandy Powell), Best Art Direction/Set Decoration (including Jill Quertier), Best Picture (including Donna Gigliotti).

Jenny Shircore wins an Oscar and a BAFTA for Best Makeup on *Elizabeth* (1998, Shekhar Kapur). The film is nominated for a further six Oscars. At the BAFTAs, Elizabeth wins another five awards, including Best Performance by an Actress in a Leading Role (Cate Blanchett), and is nominated for a further six.

1997　Ann Roth wins an Oscar for Best Costume Design in *The English Patient* (1996, Anthony Minghella).

1997     Stella Bruzzi's book *Undressing Cinema: Clothing and Identity in the Movies* published.

1996     *Antonia* (directed by Marleen Gorris) wins an Oscar for Best Foreign Language film

1994     Jane Campion becomes the first woman to win the Palme d'Or at the Cannes Film Festival with *The Piano*. The film also wins three Oscars (Best Actress in a Leading Role, Best Supporting Actress, Best Writing – Original Screenplay) and is nominated for a further five Oscars (and numerous other awards), including Best Director.

        Jackie Stacey's book *Star Gazing: Hollywood Cinema and Female Spectatorship* published.

1989     Jane Campion's film *Sweetie* released.

1987     Christine Gledhill's edited collection *Home Is Where the Heart Is: Studies in Melodrama and the Woman's Film* published.

        Vivienne Verdoe Roe wins an Oscar for Best Documentary, Short Subjects for her film *Women – for America, for the World* (1986)

1986     Charlotte Brunsdon's edited collection of essays *Films for Women* published.

1984     Mary Ann Doane, Patricia Mellencamp and Linda Williams's *Re-vision: Essays in Feminist Film Criticism* published.

1982     Mary Ann Doane's article 'Film and the Masquerade: Theorising the Female Spectator' published in the journal Screen.

1981     Laura Mulvey's article 'Afterthoughts on "Visual Pleasure and Narrative Cinema" inspired by King Vidor's *Duel in the Sun* (1946)' published in Framework.

1979     Sally Potter's feminist theory film *Thriller* released.

        The first female Prime Minister in Britain elected – Margaret Thatcher

1977     Laura Mulvey's film *Riddle of the Sphinx* continues her work with Peter Wollen in making feminist theory films.

1976     The Domestic Violence Act (UK) attempts to increase the Courts' protection of battered wives and gives police powers of arrest for breaching an injunction in cases of domestic violence.

1975     Laura Mulvey's essay 'Visual Pleasure and Narrative Cinema' published in Screen.

1975    *Work of Dorothy Arzner: Towards a Feminist Cinema* (ed Claire Johnston) published.

1974    *Penthesilea, Queen of the Amazons* by Laura Mulvey (co-directed with Peter Wollen) puts feminist theory into practice.

Jump Cut, quarterly journal with a feminist perspective, launched.

Contraceptives free for all women on the NHS.

Molly Haskell's book *From Reverence to Rape: The Treatment of Women in the Movies* published.

1973    Claire Johnston's 'Women's Cinema as Counter Cinema' in Johnston's *Notes on Women's Cinema* published, first anthology of feminist film theory.

Season of Women's Cinema at the National Film Theatre, London.

Toronto Women and Film Festival.

*Popcorn Venus: Women, Movies and the American Dream*, by Marjorie Rosen, the first book on women and film, published.

1972    Film Comment publishes a filmography of women directors.

Special women's event at the Edinburgh Film Festival.

Take One, Film Library Quarterly and Velvet Light Trap journals all have special features on women and film.

New York International Festival of Women's Films.

The American journal Women and Film launched. Its editors see themselves as feminist activists. Focus within the journal upon women's oppression in the industry, representation and film theory.

1971    Release of the first generation of feminist documentary films including: *Growing up Female*, *Janie's Janie*, *Three Lives* (produced by Kate Millet) and *The Woman's Film*.

1970    Demonstration against the Miss World competition.

Major second-wave feminist texts are published, signaling a shift towards feminist theory as political practice. Landmark texts include: Shulamith Firestone's *Dialectic of Sex: The Case for Feminist Revolution*, Kate Millet's *Sexual Politics* and Germaine Greer's *The Female Eunuch*.

The Equal Pay Act demands that equal pay for men and women doing the same job had to be brought in within five years.

1969    The Divorce Reform Act (implemented in 1971), broadens the grounds for divorce.

1968   Demonstration against the Miss America contest.

1967   The Abortion Act (UK), makes abortion easier, as it enables social as well as medical grounds to be allowed.

1964   The Married Women's Property Act (UK).

1963   Betty Friedan 's book *The Feminine Mystique* published, in which she focuses upon the feminism of the past.

Anne V Coates wins an Oscar for Best Film Editing for *Lawrence of Arabia* (1962, David Lean).

1960   The Contraceptive Pill is introduced in England and America.

Elizabeth Haffenden wins an Oscar for Best Costume Design (Colour) for her work on *Ben Hur* (1959, William Wyler).

1949   Simone de Beauvoir's book *The Second Sex* published, exploring the ways in which Woman is constructed as Other within culture.

1945   The Family Allowance Act (UK), begins a state system of Child Benefits that were to be paid directly to mothers.

1930   Welfare Centres (UK) allowed to give birth control advice to married women.

1928   The Equal Franchise Act (Flapper's Vote) (UK) gives all women over 21 the vote.

1923   The Matrimonial Causes Act (UK) makes the grounds for divorce the same for men and women.

1922   Dorothy Arnzer's *Blood and Sand* released. Arnzer is to become the most prominent female director of the era.

1920   In the book *Careers for Women*, Ida May Park writes the chapter on directing.

1918   Representation of the People Act (UK) passed before the end of World War I. For the first time some women can vote – if they are over 30 and a householder, or if they are the wife of a local government elector.

1914   Lois Weber, who owns her own studio, actively promotes other women. She encourages Cleo Madison and Dorothy Davenport to direct, hires Frances Marion, who is to become the most renowned female scriptwriter of the 20th century, and becomes a life-long friend of Mary Pickford.

1913   The first martyr in the campaign for women's suffrage, Emily Wilding Davidson, dies after throwing herself under the King's horse in the Derby.

1912     The Vitagraph actress Helen Gardner, forms her own production company in New York, and makes a dozen feature films under her own banner.

1910     Alice Guy forms Solax in New Jersey, America and supervises several hundred films over the next four years.

1897     National Union of Women's Suffrage Societies, the first national suffrage movement, is formed. Millicent Fawcett is the President.

1896     Alice Guy becomes one of the first film directors. She is a secretary in Paris to the Gaumonts, who agree to let her 'play' with their cameras as long as her clerical duties do not suffer. She is to become the head of their production company.

This timeline is available as a student handout at www.bfi.org.uk/tfms.

# The industry

## • Director as male 'creator'

Filmmaking is a highly collaborative process, involving vast numbers of people working behind the scenes, to take a film from script to screen. Yet despite the numbers of people involved, it is the director who is usually given the most recognition and status, and is seen to be in control of the creative vision of the film. This creative vision is usually seen to be male.

Steven Spielberg, Martin Scorsese, Francis Ford Coppola, Quentin Tarantino, James Cameron and John Woo have all become household names. The mass media promote such directors like superstars: from books and magazine articles to posters and trailers promoting the film by using the power of their names. They occupy the spotlight often as much as the stars in front of the camera at awards ceremonies, promotional interviews and 'The making of ...' documentaries.

The rise of DVD has raised the profile and status of the director even higher, with special 'Director's Cut' editions revealing how the film was originally envisaged as a product before it was changed, cut or reformatted to ensure the widest appeal and box-office return. The director's commentary on DVDs provides an exclusive glimpse into his/her imagination and world. As we are guided through the film, we become closer to understanding the magical creative process that has taken place.

This 'magical process' can be seen to be coded as male. While women have been, since the early days of cinema, an integral part of the filmmaking process as stars, editors, screenplay writers and costume designers (among many other roles), they have mainly been in a position where they served under men, 'helping them realise their visions' (Quart 1989: 2). As directors, though, 'women have been virtually invisible' (Mayne 1984: 51). According to Barbara Quart:

> One statistic has it that between 1949 and 1979 (and this takes in the period when women started entering feature film making in numbers) one fifth of one percent of all films by American major studios were directed by women. Before that, only one woman director, Dorothy Arzner, worked in America from silents and the beginnings of sound in the 1920s into the 1940s – one woman directing in the hey day of Hollywood's productivity and power (Quart 1989: 1)

One would like to hope that things have changed more recently, but within Hollywood the proportion of female directors still remains abysmally low. According to a study by Martha M Lauzen at San Diego State University, 'women directed seven percent of the top-grossing 100 films released in 2000'. The figures for 2001, according to the study, were even lower: four per cent of the top 100 films (Goldberg 2002).

The directors who have become household names are most often male. Therefore when the term 'director' is used it has become gendered – male director is the norm. A prefix is needed – female director becomes a category, one of difference, the exception to the rule.

## • Director versus filmmaker

Although the directors of mainstream films may be raised to the status of stars, it does not always mean that they have total control over the finished product. As the writer and filmmaker Michelle Citron proposes:

> The […] problem is terminology. Director, producer/director, filmmaker … each word implies not only a particular relationship to the product and defines a different degree of control and power, but an ideology as well. (Citron 1990: 46)

In discussions of women and film, the term 'woman filmmaker' is often used, but the types of film and levels of control vary.

In principle a filmmaker has total control over the film – from original idea to directing, shooting, and editing. When a film project becomes too big for one person to control, the role shifts to one of producer and/or director. Once the budget of a film requires that the filmmaker look for outside sources of funding, then ultimately she/he no longer has total control over the production and content of the film (Citron 1990: 56).

Therefore, although the Hollywood director may have more status, they often have less control than the independent filmmaker, as they have to answer to the studio/production company bosses.

## ● Women gaining control

Within mainstream cinema, women have been given a very limited range of roles to play. Usually a woman functions within the film as erotic distraction, as sex object, damsel in distress, *femme fatale* and victim. Her role within the film is to look good and to make the male protagonist look even better. Women are rarely cast in positions of power, and if they are, they are punished for their power.

While women in film may scream, cry and orgasm very loudly, they are virtually silenced in terms of their voice within the narrative. Woman's traditional role is to be helpless, need rescuing or agree with the actions and decisions of the male protagonists.

Woman in film exists in a world of binary oppositions in which she is defined according to the 'other'. She is the good girl or the bad girl, the virgin or the whore, the 'tart with a heart' or the girl next door, the mistress or the dutiful wife. If she does not look good, then she will be punished as the bad woman. Her path to fulfilment is not brains and independence, but the love of a good man and the right hair, clothes and body.

This is not to say that these are the only representations of women, but that they are most often 'reel' representations of women constructed through the eyes and desires of the male director. They are representations that perpetuate the dominant ideologies of what women 'should' be, rather than representations of who 'real' women are.

Female stars are increasingly attempting to take control over their representation within mainstream cinema, through their involvement behind as well as in front of the camera. Stars such as Drew Barrymore, Sharon Stone, Sigourney Weaver, Jodie Foster, Sarah Jessica Parker, Christina Ricci and Sandra Bullock are just some of the women who have the credit of co-producer, executive producer, producer, or director on films in which they have starred.

Some stars are given the credit as part of their contract in order to place them in a stronger position to negotiate their representation within a film – such as the 'no nudity' clause in their contract. For some, their power and income as stars has enabled them to invest in setting up production companies for their own projects and to help others make their mark in the industry.

## ● Tips for teaching

Find out what your students already know, then you can build upon their knowledge, and they will be more involved and enthusiastic.

So start with **Worksheets 1**, **2** and **3**.

- **Worksheet 1** encourages students to reflect upon their film likes and dislikes. This not only acts as a useful icebreaker exercise, but also gives you a chance to find out more. I tend to use this at the start of the course (and keep a copy from each student), and at the end of the course ask students to do the exercise again and reflect upon whether their tastes have changed.

- **Worksheet 2** helps students to reflect upon the names they know in the film industry – how many are male and how many are female for each category? Ask students to collect and present data, treat the discussions as a 'sample group' and discuss and analyse the findings.

- **Worksheet 3** helps students to reflect upon representations of stars in the media and the types of roles that they play within their films.

worksheet ① **Passionate about film?**

Working on your own, make notes on the following questions.

Name five films that you love.
1
2
3
4
5

Name five films that you hate.
1
2
3
4
5

What is it about these films that you like/dislike the most?

Which film genre do you dislike the most and why?

Page 1 of 4 · Women and Film

1 of 4 pages

worksheet ② **Names in the film industry – men versus women**

Working in small groups, spend 5–10 minutes brainstorming and making notes of names of individuals (past and present) in the film industry, in front of and behind the camera. Use extra sheets if needed.

| Name of individual | Role(s) – eg star, director, producer cinematographer, costume designer | Male (M) or female (F) |
| --- | --- | --- |
| | | |

Page 1 of 2 · Women and Film

1 of 2 pages

worksheet ③ **Stars and typecasting**

Through media representations in film, television, magazines, newspapers, radio and the internet, we believe that we 'know' stars. We find out details not only of the characters they play in their films, but also of what we believe to be the 'real' person.

- Working in pairs or small groups, spend 10–15 minutes discussing and making notes on the questions below. Then present your findings to the class.

Choose **20 female stars** and write their names against the numbers below.

1
2
3
4
5
6
7
8
9
10
11
12
13
14
15
16
17
18
19
20

- Now write the number of each star in one or more of the categories below.

| Bimbo | Sexy |
| --- | --- |
| Powerful | Private |
| Strong | Intelligent |
| Best-dressed | Worst-dressed |
| Most beautiful/most desirable/'best' body | Least beautiful/least desirable/'worst' body |
| Star(s) you most admire | Star(s) you least admire |

- Discuss with your group why you think the stars fit into these categories.
- Discuss and analyse your findings with the rest of the class.
- Provide a written summary of the stars that the class agreed upon in each category (if any).
- Identify any stars which students don't agree about and discuss why there are disagreements?
- Was there a significant difference in the choices by the male students compared to the female students?

Page 1 of 1 · Women and Film

1 page

19

Students enjoy discussing stars; they dominate the mass media – not just film magazines such as Empire and Total Film, but also women's and men's magazines, the press and advertising. While it may not be the most academic discussion initially, students will have an opinion and it will get them talking.

Ideally you want this discussion to lead to a debate about why they know so much about female stars and so little about women behind the camera. From this point you can start to introduce the ways of investigating women and film.

## Theoretical developments

### ● The category 'Woman'

The rise of second-wave feminism in the 1960s and 1970s, and also during the 1970s of feminist film theory, led to calls for a fuller understanding of what it meant to live in the category 'Woman'.

As Sue Thornham discusses, 'Woman' is trapped in a difficult relationship between three central figures:

1. The figure of 'Woman' as 'image or cinematic representation';
2. The figure of the real-life woman – actual women, people within history and culture;
3. The figure of the feminist theorist who 'speaks as a woman' (Thornham 1997: ix–x).

It is therefore very important when teaching women and film (and the representation of women across the mass media) that you ensure that students understand that 'Woman' exists both as a construction and a reality, and one does not always reflect the other. The mediation of the image of Woman is central to all analyses within women and film.

A physical woman may perform woman as an image, but often she has no voice in her construction. The image of woman is also often constructed as an idealised (and often highly sexualised) image for the male gaze. 'Woman' therefore comes to represent not one person of the female sex, but a category – a category that is ultimately defined as 'Other' to men.

### ● The absence of 'Woman' in culture and history

As a category, Woman appears to have been written out of history. It is not that there have been no 'important' women within history, but that they have been marginalised. In constructing a social history of popular culture, half of the human race has been ignored.

In film, women worked under men in roles deemed to be less important, such as scriptwriting or costume design. Or they were the muses, wives or lovers seeming to have no impact or input other than to inspire the creative vision of the male.

## ● Feminism and the battle to find Woman's voice in culture

Woman had no public voice in the language of culture and politics. In turn women were encouraged to become activists, to fight against their oppression and their silencing by patriarchal culture.

This 'fight' took two forms:

1. Against the constructed image of Woman – for instance, the demonstrations against the Miss World contest in 1970;
2. Against the ways in which Woman had been excluded in history and theoretical writings, and in turn writing 'her-story' to place the experiences of women into history.

Key to this fight was the development of two key areas: feminist film theory and feminist film production.

Feminist film theory attempted to:

- Analyse and critique the constructed image of Woman within film by men for a male spectator;
- Attack the celebration in film theory of the work of the great male auteurs (such as Alfred Hitchcock, Douglas Sirk and John Ford) by reclaiming the 'lost' history of women's involvement in film production;
- Place Woman into the cinema, both as a theoretical spectator (constructed by the text) and as a physical member of the audience.

Feminist film production attempted to:

- Apply feminist film theory to create a new language of filmmaking, to explore the construction of woman as object and deconstruct the pleasures of mainstream narrative cinema;
- Place women back into history through documenting their experiences.

It is important to remember that this was not the first time that feminists had explored Woman's place in history. During the period between the end of the nineteenth and the early twentieth centuries a first wave of political action and theoretical writing emerged. One can argue that during this first wave, the political action of the women's movement (such as that of the Suffrage campaigners), was distinct from the theoretical work of feminist writers, such as Virginia Woolf and Simone de Beauvoir, with their writings on issues of female subjectivity, the role of women and women's cultural production.

It was not until second-wave feminism that women (such as Laura Mulvey) combined the theoretical work of feminism and politics of the women's movement with the practice of filmmaking.

## ● Women re-imaging history

The 1970s saw women forming independent distribution and filmmaking groups and organising women's film festivals. Women began to gain access to production, in order to critique and redress the existing systems of representation of women and rewrite the conventional history (see Thornham 1997). As Michelle Citron discusses, in the United States, 'documentaries were seen by feminists as the politically appropriate film form' (Citron 1990: 50). This film form with its cheaper, mobile equipment allowed 'outsiders' into the world of film production in order to tell their stories.

### *Example*

Documentaries such as Connie Field's *The Life and Times of Rosie the Riveter* (1980) were key to such politicised work in reclaiming women's history. The film gives a voice to those women who formed an industrial workforce during World War II. Using the documentary technique of 'talking heads', the film moves women out of the private sphere into the public sphere. The film attempts to tell the real story of these women, their actual experiences, which increasingly as the film progresses conflict with the official male-centred propaganda history of World War II.

## ● Tips for teaching

See **Worksheet 4.**

Possibly a difficult one to tackle with less mature students, but try to encourage students to think about what is and is not shown in representations of women in the mass media. What aspects of women's lives are hidden, not given narrative time? What are the taboo aspects of women's lives? In what types of media text do we see the work of femininity? Upon what types of women do documentaries tend to focus?

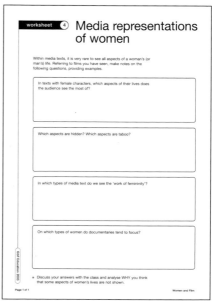

1 page

# The rise of counter cinema

Documentary may have been an important tool for telling women's stories, but it also came under criticism from feminist theorists. Claire Johnston's 'Women's Cinema as Counter Cinema' (1973, reprinted in Thornham 1999) was key in critiquing the role that the realist aesthetic played in the construction of stereotypes of women. Woman has been constructed in mainstream cinema through the male gaze. She exists as spectacle, as object to be looked at. She is silenced; she is spoken for, existing only for the satisfaction of the male hero.

Claire Johnston argued that in order for feminist cinema to be truly effective it must become a counter cinema. Only by confronting the accepted representations of reality in film could feminists expose their falseness.

## ● So what is counter cinema?

Countercinema, as Susan Hayward discusses, 'is a cinema that, through its own cinematic practices, questions and subverts existing cinematic codes and conventions' (Hayward 1996: 58). Essentially it deconstructs the language of mainstream narrative film. This is cinema that draws attention to itself as construction. The illusion of the projection of light onto the screen as enabling us to escape into another three-dimensional world is shattered.

For instance:

- There is no safe narrative: no simple beginning, middle and end, no happy ever after resolution and closure.
- The continuity of space and time is disrupted.
- Settings are not naturalistic, but draw attention to themselves as background and setting.

### Sally Potter's Thriller (1979)

This film is much quoted within writings on feminist film production and rightly so. It is a reworking of the opera *La Bohème* and tells the story of Mimi, the woman who dies. The film resists dominant cinematic techniques by giving us no opening credits, no establishing shots. The *mise en scène* of the attic is dominated by a flatness resembling the sets on a stage. There is an absence of naturalistic lighting; instead, the set is dominated by shadows and darkness. There is little explanation of Mimi's actions. Still images are intercut with music and moving images. When she speaks, she speaks in French. Tableaux freeze the narrative action. There is an absence of close-ups in order to 'read' facial expressions. There are no reaction shots or point-of-view camera work.

## ● The problem with counter cinema

Sally Potter's *Thriller* is literally 'the' textbook example of countercinema; it can be seen as the practical application of feminist film theory. When I saw it, I was left in no doubt as to what was meant by the deconstruction of film language. It is hard work; there is no obvious pleasure. It does not sweep us into a narrative where we escape into another world. While the film is 'interesting' from a theoretical and academic perspective, it refuses the pleasures of cinema.

The deconstruction of film language created problems with the very audiences it was meant to empower, who instead were alienated by it. While mainstream narrative cinema is problematic in terms of the representation of women and pleasures for the female spectator, it still retained pleasures for the real women who watched mainstream films.

## ● Tips for teaching

See **Worksheet 5**.

Investigate the types of narrative structure that students consume. How adventurous are they with narrative? Are they prepared to watch texts that make them think, that are hard work? What elements of film language do they place as having the most importance?

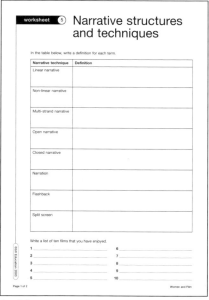

1 of 2 pages

# Allowing pleasure

Since the 1980s, feminist film (and media) theory has shifted from a concern with addressing the representation of women, and woman's place in history, to an exploration of the pleasures of mass media texts. This has included a re-reading of mainstream texts and an exploration of how they offer pleasures for the female spectator.

During the 1970s, the representation of woman as 'object' in the mass media was seen to be central to women's oppression. In turn, one could argue that to be 'a feminist' women had to resist the 'most objectionable form of commodity fetishism' and the urge, as Pamela Church Gibson discusses, to 'present and display themselves in order to gratify male desire' (1998: 36). Thus make-up, high heels and a glamorised image of self were seen to be wrong as they constructed and represented women 'for' men.

Despite this, many women found pleasures in romantic fiction, make-up and fashion etc, yet still regarded themselves as adhering to the political agendas of feminism. In turn this led to the notion of guilty pleasures, those that a 'feminist' ought not to admit to for they were deemed to be too frivolous.

## ● Pleasures and the mainstream

Central to the notion of guilty pleasure is the dichotomy between enjoyment and feeling as if one is doing something 'bad'. That which is popular and mainstream, whether it be film, television, music, or print, may not feel as 'worthy', as its focus is entertainment and pleasure, rather than attempting to inform, educate and challenge its audience. One can argue that representations of women in film can raise such feelings of guilty pleasure. For instance, we may feel that Ripley in the *Alien* films (1979, 1986, 1992, 1997), or Sarah Conner in *Terminator 2: Judgement Day* (1991), provide stronger, more worthy representations of women than say the *Charlie's Angels* films (2000 and the sequel *Charlie's Angels: Full Throttle*, 2003, both starring Cameron Diaz, Drew Barrymore and Lucy Liu). Ripley and Sarah Conner are arguably stronger, tougher, far less concerned with looking glamorous than the stars of *Charlie's Angels*. Yet Ripley and Sarah Conner can be seen as too tough, too butch, too much a gendered role reversal. Many women may not want to be seen as objects or bimbos, but also don't want to be too masculinised. The *Charlie's Angels* films can be seen to epitomise the notion of guilty pleasure, they attempt to be nothing more than escapist entertainment, adventures starring beautiful and glamorous women who can also high kick and perform the role of the action hero. What is interesting about the *Charlie's Angels* films, is not whether or not they can be regarded as feminist texts, but the pleasures that they attempt to offer and the ways in which the audience engages with the films. What do both men and women enjoy about the text? Does it inspire copying, consumption and role-play?

Thus media consumption is not a passive activity, but one in which we select elements of the text in order to gratify our needs, desires and emotions. One can argue that we select different texts based upon our moods and what we want to gain from it. While the pleasures of watching glamorous women may be relegated to the realm of guilty pleasure, one needs to ask why some of us feel guilty at all?

When exploring pleasure, you should encourage your students to reflect upon their own consumption and to create their own pieces of audience research – maybe a focus group to explore the pleasures of contemporary media.

By investigating the patterns of consumption of real audiences and the pleasures that they seek, you can in turn explore the ways in which media texts can be seen to construct texts that attempt to offer those pleasures. See **Worksheet 6**.

While this guide focuses upon women and film, it is also very useful when exploring pleasure and consumption to take an intertextual approach and to also study television programmes that centre upon female characters. As suggested in Scheme of work 1: Industry – Audience – Genre (Week 3), *Sex and the City* can provide a useful case study for exploring female-centred narratives, representation and pleasure.

worksheet 6 — Investigating guilty pleasures

1 of 2 pages

Remember though, if using episodes of *Sex and the City*, it may be more suitable to use extracts from an episode (rather than screen a full episode), if you do not want to tackle overtly sexual material in a lesson. Series Four, Episode Two – 'The Real Me' (available on video and DVD) provides lots of interesting material for analysis (especially of constructing ideals of women in the fashion industry) with Carrie being asked to star as a 'real person' alongside models in a New York-style fashion show.

See www.bfi.org.uk/tfms for a case study on *Sex and the City*: a mainstream 'feminist' text or perpetuating patriarchal ideologies?

● **Negotiated pleasures**

Central to contemporary feminist media, film and cultural theories of pleasure, is a focus upon the notion of negotiation. Meaning is not fixed, but rather is tied to moments of:

1.  Production – where meaning is encoded;
2.  The text – creating a meaningful discourse;
3.  Reception – where meaning is decoded.

While certain meanings may be encoded into a text, the pleasures of a text will always be dependent upon the decoding of meaning by the audience. The reading of a text is subject to the context of reception by the individual based upon historical, social and cultural differences. A text may have preferred meanings, depending on a culture's dominant ideologies, but, by the time the text is decoded by audiences, a process of negotiation has taken place in which meaning may be stripped of its original connotations. Just because a member of the audience may gain pleasures from a text does not automatically mean that they subscribe to its dominant ideologies. Rather than focus purely upon the ways in which texts construct meaning for an imaginary spectator, feminist theorists increasingly became interested in the ways in which real audiences use texts.

# 3

# Case studies

## Introduction

In this section, three case studies are provided, examining different yet intertwining aspects of women and film:

- Women working in the film industry;
- Stars, representation and audience pleasures;
- Genre, representation and media language – Heritage and Post-heritage film and costume analysis.

As discussed in the introduction, you should try wherever possible to integrate 'women and film' into your teaching as a matter of course and not treat it as being a token topic. In the case studies on stars and on genre the material can be used as frameworks for teaching topics without taking a 'women and film' bias. Textual case studies are provided, but you should try wherever possible to keep updating them. Use these examples as a springboard to explore new ones. Provide an overview of the theory, issues and debates for the case study, illustrate these with textual examples, then get the students to gather and present their own research. When setting essays or coursework, encourage students not to regurgitate what they have studied in class, but to discuss their case studies. It will not only keep them interested, but also demonstrate their understanding and application of the debates/issues.

Also see ideas for further development work, at the end of each of the case studies.

## CASE STUDY 1: Women working in the film industry

This case study provides a springboard for studying women working in the film industry. While it is useful for students to have knowledge of the history of women working in film and of independent, avant-garde or feminist film production, it is more accessible and relevant in terms of the specifications for students to study women currently working in the industry.

This case study is therefore divided into three parts:

● Statistics on women's employment in mainstream film – using Martha M Lauzen's *The Celluloid Ceiling*;
● Supporting women working in the film industry – the role of Women in Film and Television (WFTV);
● No place for a woman – Kathryn Bigelow and the action genre.

## 1 Statistics on women's employment in mainstream film

In her study *The Celluloid Ceiling: Behind-the-Scenes Employment of Women in the Top 250 Films of 2001*, Martha M Lauzen found that:

> 'Overall, women comprised 19 per cent of executive producers, producers, directors, writers, cinematographers, and editors working on the top 250 domestic grossing films of 2001.' (Lauzen 2002)

A year later, in her study of the top 250 films of 2002, the figures had dropped even lower, from 19 per cent in 2001, to 17 per cent in 2002 (Lauzen 2003).

**Comparison of percentage of women employed in top 100 and top 250 films of 2002**

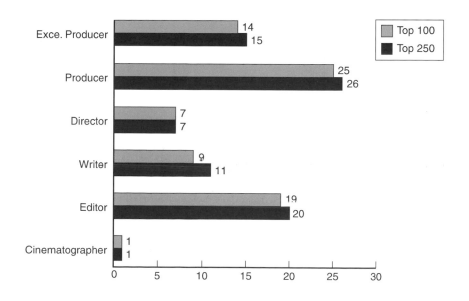

Source: http://www.moviesbywomen.com/stats2003.html#fig1

## Historical comparison of percentage of women employed behind the scenes on top 250 films

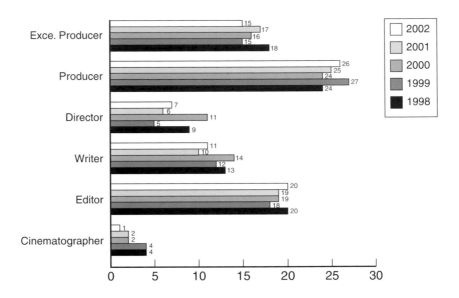

Source: http://www.moviesbywomen.com/stats2003.html#fig2

## Historical comparison of percentage of women employed behind the scenes on top 100 films

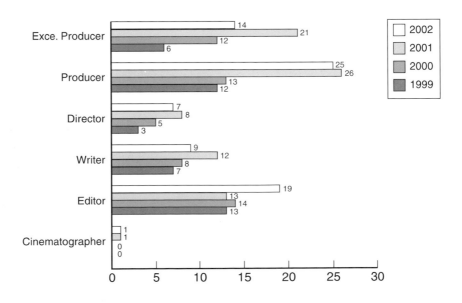

Source: http://www.moviesbywomen.com/stats2003.html#fig3

### Worrying trends

According to Lauzen, while the number of women producers increased, between 1998 and 2002, there was a decline in the percentages of women executive producers, directors, writers, and cinematographers (Lauzen 2003).

### What does a producer do?

Skillset's* *A–Z of Jobs in the Audio Visual Industries* states that essentially 'producers 'manage' the production and bring together all the elements to make a film [...] work, such as finance, cast and crew.' (Skillset *A–Z*: 65)

All producing occupations according to Skillset require the following knowledge and skills:

- Excellent communication and interpersonal skills, with the ability to give and accept direction as required and work well with others;
- Organisation, research and planning skills;
- Health and safety knowledge and awareness;
- Willingness to work long and irregular hours;
- Knowledge of law as it affects the media, including copyright and compliance.

While some producer roles do include the creative visualisation of ideas, the role can (often) be seen to be more organisational in nature. Producers are responsible for 'acquiring the human, financial and technical resources needed to realise creative ideas' (Skillset A–Z: 65).

While by no means dismissing the very important role of the producer, it remains true that, with the low numbers of women working as directors, men are in control of the creative vision, with women working to support and organise them.

### What about editors?

According to Lauzen (2003), between 1992 and 2002, there has been a modest gain from 14 to 19 per cent in the number of women editors employed on the top 100 films.

It is the editor's role to liase with the director to decide 'which of the many "takes" of a particular shot is the right one to use' (Gates 1995: 35) and reassemble the images into sequences that are 'so smooth, so seemingly seamless' that the audience is quite unaware that they are 'actually watching a series of shots, which may even have been filmed in different places and at different times' (Gates 1995: 36). According to Robert Angell, 'a good editor can certainly improve an actor's performance and enliven a routine script but cannot change radically a bad basic idea' (2002: 45).

---

*Skillset is the national training organisation for broadcast, film, video and interactive media in the UK: www.skillset.org.

A key figure within the American film industry is Thelma Schoonmaker, with an editing career that has (to date) spanned five decades. However, she is frequently defined in terms of her relationships with men, including her marriage to director, Michael Powell, and her working relationship with Martin Scorsese. While Schoonmaker has worked with other directors, including Allison Anders for *Grace of My Heart* (1996), her work has been dominated by her collaborations with Scorsese since his first feature *Who's That Knocking at My Door* (1968). She believes that the working relationship between the editor and the director is crucial. It is a relationship of trust, friendship and backbreaking hard work to refine and create rhythms that work within the film.

● **Tips for teaching**

David Morgan's interview with Schoonmaker for the website 'Wide Angle/Closeup' provides an excellent springboard for exploring the teamwork required between the editor and director and for investigating how the status of the auteur director is perpetuated.

http://members.aol.com/morgands1/closeup/text/cfthelm2.htm

**Virtually absent:**

According to Lauzen, 22 per cent of the 'films released in 2002 employed no women directors, executive producers, producers, writers, cinematographers, or editors' (Lauzen 2003). The percentage of women cinematographers in the top 250 films was a meagre two per cent in both 2000 and 2001 (Lauzen 2002). In 2002 though, the figure had dropped even lower: women comprised only one per cent of all cinematographers working on the top 250 and 100 films' (Lauzen 2003).

*What does a cinematographer do?*

Cinematography is a creative and interpretive process that culminates in an original work. Basically, the cinematographer is the Director of Photography for a given film. He or she is an expert on photographic processes, lighting and manipulation of the camera. The cinematographer is concerned with frame composition, aspect ratio (ratio of frame width to frame height), camera position (angle, level, height, distance), film stock and its treatment during post-production, film speed, rate of shooting, and choice of camera lens. What we see on the movie screen is a direct result of the cinematographer's vision (Bradley 2001). It is both a highly creative and a very technical role, which relies on the ability to liaise between the producer and the director in capturing each shot on film.

● **Tips for teaching**

You should encourage your students to reflect and discuss why they think there are so few women working in technical roles in the film industry. The following sources may be useful:

- The executive summaries of Lauzen's *Celluloid Ceiling* studies on the employment of women in film in the top 250 grossing films (in America) of 2000, 2001, and 2002 are available online at: www.moviesbywomen.com/stats.html

- In her study of films from 2002 (published in 2003) Lauzen analyses the statistics of not only women working behind the camera, but also those 'on screen'.

- For an analysis of the number of women working in American prime-time television, the executive summary of Lauzen's *Boxed in: Women on Screen and Behind the Scenes in the 2001–2002 Prime-Time Season* is available on the Movies by Women website at: www.moviesbywomen.com/stats2002.html. The executive summary is useful for a media industries case study on employment and as institutional information to support work on analysing American situation comedies and dramas.

- For further reading on the different roles in the film industry, see Skillset's *A–Z of Jobs in the Audio Visual Industries*. The document is available online at http://www.skillset.org/careers/home.asp (approx. 100 pages in total).

**Worksheet 7** encourages students to develop a profile of a woman working in a specific role behind the camera. This could be developed into a piece of coursework.

1 page

## 2 Supporting women working in the film industry

### *The impact of digital technology*

With the rise of digital technology, filmmaking equipment is increasingly more accessible both financially and physically. The technology to produce films is available on the high street, with digital non-linear editing software enabling filmmakers (potentially) to edit on PCs at home. The portability of hand-held cameras provides liberation from the physical limitations (and bruises) of heavier equipment. Such freedom, as was demonstrated with Danny Boyle's *28 Days Later* (2002), enables cameras literally to be taken to the streets, to create a new language of visual expression.

For the scenes in London in *28 Days Later*, 10–15 cameras were used in order to record what would become only two minutes of footage. Danny Boyle (2002) has argued that he wanted the scenes to 'feel like the camera was wandering through the city'. For Boyle, digital video (DV) offers several advantages: it is easy and quick to use, is accident friendly and can be ready to shoot very quickly. DV may not have the definition of film, but Boyle loves the urban beauty of the images. The cameras suit shooting in cities, and 'these are the cameras we use for shooting reality'.

Digital films can be distributed and viewed worldwide via the internet. Websites such as Kevin Spacey's TriggerStreet.com offer:

> 'an interactive mechanism for the purpose of discovering and showcasing new and unique talent. Based on the principles of creative excellence, it provides industry access and exposure to help build the careers of notable new filmmakers and screenwriters of our day.'
> (About Us: *www.triggerstreet.com*)

Such technology and initiatives provide new opportunities for women wanting to move into filmmaking, but there are also limitations:

- **Visual style** – DV is more 'gritty' than celluloid, creating a different look to the film;
- **The viewing experience** – if films are distributed via the internet, then the majority of the audience will be watching them on their PC monitors, rather than on the 'big screen' of the cinema;
- **Money and control** – while DV may keep the budget low and the control high, directors without major financial support are less likely to achieve commercial success and become A-list.

Therefore, while digital technology may help women to realise their creative visions and create a new way of expression, as Jane Cussons, Chief Executive of WFTV posits, 'will digital films ever be so fantastic' as celluloid? (2003) As a result, women need support in order to make the leap from independent filmmaking to mainstream cinema production.

### An 'ego job'

According to Cussons, directing can be seen as an 'ego job'. She was told by Alan Parker that a good director needs a 'steel backbone', and she was left wondering whether really what he meant was that you need 'balls'. A director, she argues, needs to be able to 'be strong' in order to manage a cast and crew. Women are often seen to be too 'soft, vulnerable and emotional' and in turn not able to handle the pressures of the role of the director (Cussons 2003).

If only six per cent of the top 250 grossing films (and four per cent of the top 100 films) of 2001 were directed by women, then the majority of mainstream cinema releases are the visions of men. Chick flicks and romantic comedies may provide opportunities for the representation of 'female experiences', but they are usually discussed as 'women's films'. Thus the battle is for women to move not only into mainstream cinema, but also into a wider range of genres, in order to provide a different viewpoint on the world.

### Supporting women working in the industry

In January 2003, Freshminds Ltd, London, were commissioned by Women in Film and Television (WFTV) to produce a report on the position of women employed within the film and TV industry in the UK. The brief of the project was to identify issues on which the organisation can campaign through lobbying and public relations activities (Freshminds Ltd 2003: 4)

While women make up 50 per cent of those working in broadcast television, they only make up 15 per cent of those employed in 'films in production' in the UK (Freshminds Ltd 2003: 7). According to the report (2003: 9) women comprise:

- 93 per cent of all hair and make-up artists;
- 83 per cent of all costume and wardrobe jobs.

While women dominate these roles, there are very limited job opportunities for them (whether freelance or permanent). Echoing the trends within Lauzen's American study, Freshminds Ltd found that women in the UK film and television industries are under-represented in the technical areas:

- Lighting – only eight per cent are women;
- Broadcast engineering and cinema projectionist – only nine per cent are women;
- Camera – only 10 per cent are women;
- Sound – only 11 per cent are women.

According to the report, this trend starts during the training stages of women's careers, where women do not favour sound, lighting or cinematography.

### ● Tips for teaching

You could invite your students to discuss possible reasons why women seem to show a lack of enthusiasm for technical roles. To what extent are women put off technical roles? Why? Where does this happen?

The report proposes that possible reasons may include:

- The need for a high level of computer/technical expertise;
- The heavy manual aspect to location work, especially for lighting;
- The male-dominated environment.
  (Freshminds Ltd 2003: 12-13)

According to Cussons, there is a perception in the industry that gender has been 'done' as an important diversity issue (2003). Instead, the focus of equal opportunities has shifted to issues of race, ethnicity and sexuality.

Filmmaking can be seen as a 'boys' club', one in which the main positions of power are occupied by men. Director Tara Veneruso argues that the process of moving from a short film to pitching your idea for a major feature film is usually undertaken over drinks at film festival parties (quoted in Goldberg 2002). As Michelle Goldberg argues, while this process is fine if you are a member of the 'boys' club', for women 'chatting up an older man over drinks isn't construed as business – it's seen as flirting' (Goldberg 2002). Thus women are often placed on the outside of the casual networks where business takes place.

Although ideally it should be unnecessary, there is still a need for organisations that will both facilitate networking opportunities for women and provide a 'mouth-piece for gender related issues' (Cussons 2003). WFTV is one such organisation which 'exists to protect and enhance the status, interests and diversity of women working at all levels in both film, television and digital media industries' (www.wftv.org.uk). It is a non-profit-making professional association (funded through subscriptions and sponsorship) that:

- Provides a forum for industry professionals – members must have at least one year's professional experience working in television, film and/or digital media industries;
- Offers a network of contacts;
- Safeguards the interests of women working in television and film;
- Champions women's achievements in the industry.

The Chief Executive of WFTV in the United Kingdom, Jane Cussons, is quoted by the press and speaks on panel debates on women in the film/television industry, but WFTV's role is not to provide research or information. It does not 'study' or analyse women in film and television, in terms of representation issues. Therefore

- You should **not** encourage your students to contact the association expecting to be sent bundles of information that will provide easy answers to their essays and coursework on women and film.
- If you are using WFTV as a case study, it should be to discuss why such an organisation is needed. What are the advantages and disadvantages of such an association for women?

WFTV has contacts in Europe (United Kingdom, Denmark, Germany, Italy, Ireland), United States, Canada, Australia, Africa, Mexico, New Zealand and the Caribbean.

## ● No place for a woman – Kathryn Bigelow and the action genre

Kathryn Bigelow is one female director who has managed the leap into the mainstream. In fact, she can be seen to be **the** A-list female director. She is most well known for:

- *K-19: The Widowmaker* (2002)
- *Strange Days* (1995)
- *Point Break* (1991)
- *Blue Steel* (1990)

See *www.imdb.co.uk* for a more detailed filmography and other information.

Kathryn Bigelow

Not only is she one of a 'handful of big budget female filmmakers' (Waters 2002), but she works within what is perceived to be the 'masculine' genre of action, rather than the stereotypically 'feminine' genres of romantic comedy and chick flicks.

As Jane Cussons argues: 'Most of the big-grossing films are full of special effects, they are big-budget blockbusters and for some reason women are not considered suitable for this. [...] Kathryn Bigelow is probably the only one accepted at doing this sort of thing.' (Cussons quoted in Waters 2002)

Bigelow's films, though, are by no means formulaic genre pieces – they can be seen to combine 'an affinity for the frenetic rhythms of the thriller with a taste for subversive genre bending' (Hultkrans 1995: 79). As Andrew Hultkrans argues, Bigelow is 'a consummate technician whose balletic action sequences remind us how cinematically pure the language of violence can be'.

Yvonne Tasker states that Bigelow's films are 'marked by a strong sense of visual style – careful composition and lighting and an eye for iconography'. While her work is dominated by visual excess, it is not purely style over substance. Her work explores character and emotions with an intensity rarely seen within the action genre. Still, Bigelow's place within the Hollywood hierarchy is awkward. Her work is big budget with big-name stars. It is 'too perverse for the mainstream', yet 'not quite maverick enough' to be a major 'independent', nor 'feminist' enough to be included in several anthologies on women filmmakers. She remains 'relatively obscure, though her status as the female action director in Hollywood brings her a strange visibility' (Tasker 1999: 195–6).

### Representing the director

Bigelow's background in painting is repeatedly used in articles profiling her. Such a focus can be seen almost to 'justify' her transgression into the perceived male-dominated world of the director. She is often introduced in terms of her looks, especially her height and her poise. As Yvonne Tasker discusses, 'laid-back publicity shots serve to enhance her image'. Her long dark hair, shades, strong tailoring, jeans and leather are coupled with a 'moody expression' (Tasker 1999: 196). Bigelow is also often defined in terms of her relationship with now ex-husband James Cameron, the Hollywood A-list director, writer and producer known for his big-budget action films including *Titanic* (1997)*, Aliens* (1986) and *The Terminator* (1984).

● Encourage students to discuss **why** women filmmakers are described in terms of their image and their relationships. Is it the same for men?

In interviews with Bigelow, her position as a female director is repeatedly the subject of discussion. Arguably, the inclusion of Bigelow as a case study on female directors could risk focusing on her gender and treating her as a token case study. For me, though, while her place in the industry is crucial, what is more important is her work. She is not just a woman working in the action genre; she is a woman creating a vision that is different. Whether that difference is because she is a woman is a matter for debate.

● While it is worth noting that Bigelow works within a male-dominated genre, it is more important for students to explore **why** some genres are perceived to be masculine and some feminine. Why is it seen to be such an 'issue' that Bigelow makes action films?

Bigelow has argued that 'there's nothing more counter-productive than the notion of gender-specific filmmaking. […] I simply don't know why [action] seems to be a male domain. Character and emotionality don't always have to be relegated to quieter, more simple constructs' (Bigelow quoted in Fuller 1995: 44 and 118).

Bigelow's films are interesting because of how she constructs narratives with three-dimensional, complex (often male) characters; these both explore the spectacle of violence and action, and play with genre and the processes of spectator identification and desire.

The following films are available on DVD and VHS from major distributors.

### Textual example 1: Point Break

According to Yvonne Tasker (1993: 162), *Point Break* (1991) is a spectacular surfing movie, centring on the tense and powerful relationship that develops between FBI agent Johnny Utah (Keanu Reeves) and the charismatic leader of a group of surfing bank robbers, Bodhi (Patrick Swayze).

The film, as Tasker discusses, is conducted at a 'hectic pace', with breathtaking visuals of skydiving, surfing and car chases (1993: 162). While the action sequences are gripping, it is the representation of multiple images of masculine identity and the bubbling homoerotic desire that is central to both the narrative and the pleasures of the film.

right: Keanu Reeves in *Point Break.*

below: Keanu Reeves and Patrick Swayze in *Point Break.*

## Key points to discuss:

- The casting of Keanu Reeves and Patrick Swayze – the intertextual meanings we bring to the text and the importance of their looks and appeal for the audience;
- Father–son relationship – FBI man Pappas and Johnny Utah;
- The relationship between Bodhi and Johnny;
- The representation and display of the male body through action;
- The use of the token female to disrupt the narrative action and heterosexualise the male characters;
- The relationship between action and death.

See **Worksheet 8** for specific clips and questions for analysis.

worksheet ⑧ **Women in the film industry**

Case study: Kathryn Bigelow's *Point Break* (US, 1991)

1 of 4 pages

### *Textual example 2:* **Strange Days**

*Strange Days* (1995) represents, as Yvonne Tasker discusses, Bigelow's 'characteristic mix of elaborately crafted images and sweeping camera work with the conventions of commercial action cinema'. The film calls into question the 'implicit distinction' between:

> '**Narrative –** finding out, cause and effect, moving forward
> and
> **Visual pleasures** – contemplation, beauty, display.' (Tasker 1999: 196)

Ralph Fiennes and Angela Bassett in *Strange Days*.

In *Strange Days*, Lenny (Ralph Fiennes) deals in 'clips' – digital recordings of real-life experiences. Lenny's 'perception of reality is blurred, from hours spent 'reliving' his relationship with his ex, Faith (Juliette Lewis) through replaying the recorded memories that are the basis of his trade' (Tasker 1998: 85). In turn, the narrative of *Strange Days* self-consciously critiques the processes of voyeurism and male-centred spectator identification in mainstream cinema through positioning the spectator as an active participant/consumer of the 'clips' by using point-of-view camera work.

Through the use of the clips (especially the blackjack of Iris's rape and murder), Bigelow creates a combination of chilling violence, experimental camerawork and intense narrative involvement (Tasker 1999: 197)

**Worksheet 9** provides activities for analysing the print-based advertisements for the film, the DVD cover and the trailer. These activities help to develop student's skills in unseen text and comparative criteria analysis.

1 of 3 pages

1 of 2 pages

**Worksheet 10** provides discussion questions from selected scenes from the film that centre upon voyeurism. Please note that the film is rated 18 and that some of the scenes are graphic (sexual/violent), so make sure that you have watched it in advance to assess its suitability for your students and forewarn them, should you decide to study the film.

## Strange Days *and the buddy movie*

In addition to voyeurism, *Strange Days* also raises issues of race and gender through its appropriation of elements of the buddy movie genre.

While the film makes 'no resort to comic exchanges, the film operates in a hybrid terrain of horror, thriller, action and science fiction' (Tasker 1998: 85). The elements of the buddy movie are present through the:

● Central action/investigation partnership;
● Race and gender.

Race and gender are heavily coded within the film through the casting of Angela Bassett in the role of Mace and Ralph Fiennes in the role of Lenny. According to Bigelow, 'Mace is the narrative's moral centre [...], she is the unblemished hero' whereas Lenny is 'an anti-hero'. Mace represents 'a hard-edged reality-based component, whereas Lenny is in fantasy'. The reality disks 'tend to highlight male fantasies. Not female ones'. (Bigelow quoted in Hultkrans 1995: 104).

See **Worksheet 11**.

Key points to discuss:
● The pairing of Lenny and Mace;
● The use of masculinised costume in the representation of Mace;
● The representation of Mace as mother, and the only character to resist the pleasure of the clips;
● The representation of interracial violence in America.

Angela Bassett as Mace

1 of 3 pages

● **Ideas for development work**

*Women working in the film industry*

Case studies on:

● A specific director – mainstream/new talent, especially on non-white, non-Anglo/non-American directors;
● A female star behind the camera – eg Jodie Foster;
● A costume designer – eg Ann Roth, Sandy Powell, Kym Barrett;
● Women working in other roles behind the camera – editor, producer, cinematographer, scriptwriter, art direction, special effects.

*Kathryn Bigelow*

● Students could gather examples of advertising and marketing material for Bigelow's *K-19: The Widowmaker* and undertake a comparative critical analysis of the similarities and differences of the campaigns for *K-19* and *Strange Days*. Starting point for finding posters: www.imdb.co.uk.
● Students could undertake a comparative critical analysis of the representations of masculinity in *Point Break* and *K-19: The Widowmaker*.

# CASE STUDY 2:
## Stars, representation and audience pleasures

This case study provides a framework for the analysis of contemporary stars and the pleasures that they offer to spectators, both within and outside their films, focusing in particular on Gwyneth Paltrow.

● **Resources on stars**

There is a vast range of material, in print, in television 'documentaries' or on the web, about stars – especially Hollywood stars. Much of the material, though, is biographical, fan-based or dominated by photographs of the star on and off set. Such material can provide superb case studies for representation, but it will be highly tempting for students to lift chunks of biographical information and fan gossip and use it as 'research' for star theory. This material should be used to produce an analysis of the star image in terms of representation, as biographical information is mediated in order to construct a narrative about the stars. Students should be encouraged to use such information **as a primary source**, as a text to analyse critically, not as background information.

- ## Cultural myths and stars

See **Worksheet 12**.

These narratives often perpetuate cultural myths and in turn dominant ideologies. For instance:

- **The ugly duckling** – the star who is the geek or dork at school, who with age, diet and a stylist has become successful, beautiful etc;
- **The prom queen/cheerleader/ jock** – the star was always one of the popular crowd, won the beauty pageant, is an ex-model etc;
- **Cinderella** – the rags-to-riches fantasy – where the star from the poorest part of town is discovered by the rich and powerful executive;

worksheet 12 **Stars and cultural myths**

Through the representation of the star, media texts can be seen to perpetuate cultural myths and dominant ideologies.

**Common cultural myths**

- **The ugly duckling** – the star was the geek or the dork at school, but with age, diet and a stylist has become successful, beautiful etc.
- **The prom queen/cheerleader/ jock** – the star was always one of the popular crowd, won the beauty pageant, is an ex-model etc;
- **Cinderella** – the rags-to-riches fantasy, where the star from the poorest part of town is discovered by the rich and powerful executive;
- **The society star** – the star was from the 'right ' background with the right connections, and was always destined to make it, but will 'slum it' to prove that he/she can be like everyone else.

1 page

- **The society star** – the star is from the 'right ' background with the right connections and was always destined to make it, but will 'slum it' to prove that they can be like everyone else.

Stars, because of their sheer dominance in popular culture, are an aspect of Film/Media Studies with which students can easily engage. Your students will come with a vast array of knowledge and opinions about stars. Initially this may not be academically strong, but you should try to tap into it. Start by getting students to discuss, brainstorm and present their responses to what a star is, what they do and who are they for.

See **Worksheet 13**. Then use the key points to remember about stars to develop the discussion.

worksheet 13 **Stars and their roles**

Think about what, to you, comprise the main characteristics and roles of a star, and make notes under the following headings.

What is a star?

What qualities must a star have?

How is a star different to an actor?

What role(s) do stars serve?

Why do stars dominate magazines and tabloid newspapers so much?

Other points

1 page

# 1 Key points to remember about stars

Adapted from Richard Dyer (1999), *Stars*:

- While a star may be able to act, actors do not always become stars.
- Stars become 'public property' through the mass media – we feel as though we 'know' them and have a level of ownership over their image and believe their private lives are our business.
- What we do know about stars, we know through their representation in media texts.
- Stars are both characters in films and real people outside of film – in turn we tend to think of the star as more real and less constructed than the characters they play.
- Stars can be an investment – a means of guaranteeing income – both in terms of funding and box-office takings.
- Stars form a major portion of the budget of a film.
- Stars are used as images to sell a film – face, body, voice and personality.
- Stars act as symbols for the 'quality' of certain types of film.
- Stars are often typecast in certain roles and genres of film.
- Stars articulate social types.
- Stars' representations in the media serve to perpetuate dreams and dominant ideologies.
- Narratives provide opportunities to display the spectacle of the star.
- The close-up is essential in the creation of stardom – in order to isolate and concentrate upon looks and personality, and create intimacy between audience and star.
- The close-up also reveals the unmediated personality of the individual, and thus we can 'capture' the unique person of a performer.
- The image of the star is built up through publicity, through planted items in the media.
- Stars exist as public personalities, marketed on differences of appearance.
- Stars need to be seen in the context of their roles.
- Stars often exist as contradictions and a multiplicity of changing images.
- Stars can rise and fall in popularity.
- Stars serve to set notions of beauty and norms of attractiveness – but these are not fixed and go in and out of fashion.
- Stars are often seen to have special qualities.
- Audiences' favourite stars are often the same sex as themselves – therefore star–audience relationships are not purely based on norms of heterosexual attraction.
- The same-sex desire of audiences for stars can raise taboo issues of homosexual feeling and desire for 'straight' audiences.
- We are encouraged to identify with stars and have an emotional affinity with them. This identification sometimes extends to imitation.

- Stars are seen to have desirable lifestyles dominated by conspicuous consumption.
- Stars are sometimes perceived as ordinary people, but they are ordinary people with money and extravagant lifestyles.
- Stars can be seen to perpetuate heterosexual relations as the norm and the myth of 'love' as the ultimate relationship – more important than friendship, work, or family.

## 2 Theoretical framework

This section draws upon the theoretical work of Jackie Stacey's book *Stargazing: Hollywood Cinema and Female Spectatorship* (1994), to explore the ways in which stars enable pleasures of escapism, identification and consumption for the spectator.

### Background

Stacey's book focuses upon the relationships between audiences and stars from the 1940s and 1950s. The pleasures explored are those of the cinema-going experience and those outside the films themselves. Her book is based upon a piece of audience research. She placed an advertisement in *Woman's Weekly* and *Woman's Realm* – magazines both aimed at older women and housewives, asking women to complete a questionnaire about their cinema-going habits and the pleasures of the stars from the period. Of the women who requested a questionnaire, only 20 did not return it – an unusually high response rate. Stacey received 238 questionnaires (12 pages long), with many women adding additional sheets when describing their favourite stars. She also received 350 letters from women, as well as many diaries, scrapbooks, old photographs and leaflets. The women who responded were mostly 50 to 60 years old. The questionnaire encouraged both short and long replies and the results consisted of both the completed questionnaire and many handwritten letters, which focused on personal memories and experiences. The replies drew upon memories of stars and of the women's lives when they were in their teens to 20s, creating a popular history of stars. They drew upon women's nostalgia for the past, rather than their contemporary experiences.

Stacey's study is audience-centred, *not* text-centred. Her work is a landmark text in bridging the gap between Film Studies approaches to spectator theory and Media or Cultural Studies approaches to audiences. Feminist work on audience studies had previously tended to centre on television genres such as soap opera, and women's magazines. Feminist film studies had tended to take a very text-centred approach – examining the theoretical spectator, rather than the real person in the auditorium. Stacey is one of the first theorists to explore real audiences and stars, in relation to pleasure and consumption. She does not, however, analyse the representations of the stars within the films or within the discourses that surround the films – such as newspapers and magazines.

Stacey argues that there are three key pleasures for spectators in relation to stars: escapism, identification and consumption.

### Escapism

Many of the points Stacey raises in relation to escapism are tied to the historical contexts of the war and post-war years in Britain. When using her work to analyse contemporary cinema and stars, one therefore needs to be aware of the cultural context. She points to the following elements of escapism:

- **The cinema as dream palace** conveyed a sense of other-worldliness. The cinemas that audiences went to in the 1940s were luxurious buildings, with lavish entrances, sculptures, sweeping marble staircases, plush velvet seats and flowing swathes of fabric. They created a sense of luxury that contradicted the social realities of World War II and the post-war years.

  See **Worksheet 14**, which encourages students to investigate what has happened to the former cinemas in their area/a specific area.

1 page

- **Generating a sense of belonging.** In an age before television dominated every household, the cinema became a communal space in which audiences went to watch not only films, but also newsreels and documentaries. Several hours of viewing with intermissions enabled people to come together and share their experiences and reflect upon their viewing.

- **Escaping the war.** By creating an environment in which audiences could escape from the harsh realities of the period, the cinema became a magical place filled with dreams. Within this 'dream palace', audiences could escape social reality by watching big-budget Hollywood films. The images of glamour and sophistication that they presented differed dramatically from the rations and bomb-torn cities of Britain. This remains true even today when social realities are generally less harsh: the darkened auditorium with its projector placed behind our heads becomes the projection of our dreams, our escapist fantasies blown up upon the screen.

See **Worksheet 15** which asks students to reflect upon the experience of the cinema and how it is similar/different to other modes of consumption.

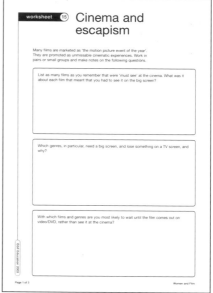

1 of 3 pages

- **Hollywood stars** were as important as the narrative of the film itself. They offered one of the key pleasures of Hollywood cinema and exist intertextually – not just in their films, but also through public appearances, signed photos from the studios, fan clubs and magazines. The audiences in Stacey's study were keen to consume the details of stars' lives that were offered to them through the studios' publicity machines.

- **Escape to Hollywood**. British stars did exist, but not on the same scale as Hollywood stars. In its images of America, Hollywood cinema offered the British spectator the possibility of another world far away from the difficulties of everyday life in Britain. Hollywood was seen to be a glamorous and luxurious world and American stars articulated ideologies of consumerism to audiences. Cinema was an affordable luxury that did not require a ration book.

- **Desirable differences**: audiences did not want images of 'ordinary' people, but of something unattainable. Stars were generally older than most of their fans and presented a more complete, confident and mature self-image. They represented an idealised image of desirability and sexual attractiveness. In female stars this was articulated through clothes, make-up, hairstyles and general physical appearance. They conveyed glamour and affluence, in stark contrast to the poverty and rationing within wartime Britain where women had to 'make do and mend'. Glamour defined femininity and was seen as something not belonging to British culture, while the unavailability of consumer goods to enable fans to become more like the star, highlighted the unattainable difference of American stars.

- **Hollywood stars offered utopian fantasies and transcendence**: the pleasure of 'losing oneself'. Audiences would become totally absorbed in the cinema experience – the darkened room and the stars on screen provided the opportunity to escape their own lives and participate in another, imaginary world for a short time.

**Worksheet 16** asks students to reflect upon the pleasures that are offered by stars. To what extent do American stars seem to be more glamorous/ more excessive than British stars?

### Identification

Identification is the process through which the spectator sympathises or engages with a character. Integral to this process is the linking of the points of view of the character and the spectator:

- **Visual point of view.** Use of camera and editing in order to build identification by seeing through the 'I' of the character.

worksheet 16 **The pleasures of stars**

Identify ten stars that you like (five female, five male) and make notes on what it is that you like most about them.

| Female star | What you like about her |
|---|---|
| | |

| Male star | What you like about him |
|---|---|
| | |

Identify what you regard to be the three most important qualities of:

| Female stars | Male stars |
|---|---|
| | |

Page 1 of 1                                 Women and Film

1 page

- **Narrative point of view.** The ways in which the character leads us through the narrative, encouraging sympathy and a sharing of knowledge.
- **Psychoanalytical theory.** Cinematic identification can also be central to the formation of gendered identities. In studying the formation of gendered and sexual identities in film and spectatorship, theorists, including Christian Metz and Laura Mulvey, have applied the work of psychoanalytic theorists such as Jacques Lacan and Sigmund Freud. The following points are useful to keep in mind:
  - E A Kaplan argues that psychoanalysis is a 'crucial tool for explaining the needs, desires and male–female positionings that are reflected in film' (White 1999: 342)
  - Rob White's section on 'Psychoanalysis' in *The Cinema Book* (341–52) provides an overview of the ways in which psychoanalysis has been applied within film theory.
  - Jacques Lacan's work on the mirror phase can be applied to the analysis of film and media texts with able students (A/B grade – especially those also undertaking AS/A2 Psychology) It can provide a framework for analysing the ways in which media texts construct images of an idealised self.
  - It can be fruitful to analyse the use of mirrors within media texts and the ways in which they not only provide idealised images, but also the destruction/distortion of images in reflections. *The Talented Mr Ripley* (1999) provides many examples of this.

The relationship between spectators and stars is often contradictory and torn between:

- **Similarity**, ie closeness to the star, enabling the spectator to recognise elements of the star in themselves and
- **Difference**, ie distance from the star, where the star can take the spectator into another world, where desires could be fulfilled.

At AS/A2 level even very able students tend to find this theoretical work very difficult. It is not needed at this level and you should avoid confusing students. The theory is only useful if they can manage to apply it.

- **Cinematic identification fantasies**

These centre upon the spectator's fantasies during the viewing of a film.

- **Devotion.** Stacey's study refers to the intense passion and attachment that spectators had for stars. For instance, one woman had seen *Calamity Jane* 45 times (Stacey 1994: 138);
- **Adoration.** The fascination develops almost to the level of fantasised romance, dominated by intense feelings;
- **Worship.** Stars are discussed in terms of a religious discourse – they become goddesses, 'out of this world' and placed at a vast spatial distance from the spectator.

The relationship between the spectator and the image of the star can create a homoerotic bond, with fantasies of:

- **Transcendence**, ultimately connected to the processes of escapism (as discussed earlier).
- **Aspiration,** when the spectator wants to be like the star, but this is impossible – the ideal always remains at a distance, unfulfilled. The desire produces longing for transformed identities.
- **Inspiration**, often associated with qualities of a person, eg strength, independence. Stars offered the audience a more powerful and confident image of self.

- **Extra-cinematic identification processes**

These take place outside the cinematic context. They involve the spectator taking part in a process of transformation to become more like the star, including:

- **Pretending** to be a character or a film star; game-playing involving the participation of other spectators.
- **Imitating**, centres upon a part of the star's identity rather than taking on the whole persona. Imitating is not just singing or dancing, but also replicating gestures and speech patterns. It focuses upon behaviour and activities. One could argue that this extends to copying of catch phrases. While male students will often vehemently deny wanting to

copy a star, many will attempt (often terrible) impressions of James Bond (always in the form of Sean Connery), action heroes, situation comedy stars, and characters from *Austin Powers*. Ask them to explore why they do this. Is it a desire for acceptance by others, to seem attractive by making others laugh?

- **Resembling** the physical appearance. Spectators select an element of self that enables a link between the star and the spectator. Star qualities become highlighted – for instance hair or eyes.

- **Copying**, also focusing on appearances – a desire to look like the stars. It is the most common form of cinematic recognition outside the cinema and centres upon the attempt to close the gap between one's own image and the idealised image of self, embodied by the star. Hairstyle is the thing most often copied, and the process does not always involve the consumption of products. Often the attempt to copy the star is accompanied by a feeling of failure.

### *Consumption*

The following points should be kept in mind:

- Consumption is culturally tied to femininity.
- Shopping encourages a connection between looking, desiring and buying. Shops can be seen as 'palaces of consumption' with their lavish displays, glass cases, and openness.
- The cinema screen can be seen as a shop window – in which luxury items are displayed for consumption by the spectator. Clothes, accessories, gadgets, cars, décor are all displayed within the film and then are available to be purchased.
- The process of consumption is becoming increasingly explicit through the use of product placement and commodity tie-ins in contemporary cinema. Products are not only subject to lingering close-ups in the films, but also featured in print and audiovisual marketing campaigns for the product. For instance:
  - Cosmetic companies including Revlon featured in *Die Another Day* and Max Factor in *Chicago*;
  - Branded mobile phones have been featured in Bond films, *The Matrix*, *Charlie's Angels*, *Lara Croft: Tomb Raider*, *Minority Report* etc.

Women not only 'have' commodities, but Woman 'is' a commodity within contemporary culture. The cinematic image is both shop window and mirror of an idealised image of femininity. To have subjectivity, she must become object. But Stacey argues that women are active in the processes of consumption. A woman uses consumption in order to construct an image of herself as an individual. The individual is constructed through the work of femininity. This requires

- **Shared knowledge.** An intimate knowledge of details of the star's commodities. Clothes and fashion are central to the attainment of feminine ideals. What was worn on screen is crucial in the transition to adult femininity. Narratives often centre upon the processes of transformation. Stars in turn represent cultural ideals of beauty. Sometimes the spectator takes on the position of the star – predicting taste and imagining her in the outfit of their choice.

- **Trademarks.** The connection between stars and specific commodities – hair, clothes, make-up, accessories. The looks of the star become images on the street to copy. For example, the trademark items of Sarah Jessica Parker as Carrie in *Sex and the City* include a flower corsage on her jackets and dresses, a wrist corsage with ribbons, an old nameplate necklace, all of which can be seen to have acted as trademark items that have been copied by spectators. Within contemporary culture, women's magazines can be seen to be instrumental in this process, presenting the spectator with 'captured' images of the star and instructions on how you, too, can copy their look. Hairstyles are central to the physical transformation of the spectator and the notion of trade marking the star. Hairstyles are often named after the star: eg women asking for a 'Rachel' after Jennifer Aniston's haircut in *Friends*.

- **Fragmentation of the body.** The whole body of the star functions as a commodity, and is also fragmented into parts:
  - **Body:** legs, breasts, bum, hair, face
  - **Face:** eyes, nose, mouth, skin
  - **Eyes:** colour, lashes, eyebrows

This fragmentation both objectifies the star and creates in the spectator a feeling of intimacy with the star. The star's body functions not only to provide ideals of feminine beauty and identity, but also to sell products to women for self-improvement.

Using **Worksheet 17**, ask students to identify and collect examples of the ways in which different stars are fragmented and commodified for consumption. *Now* magazine provides lots of examples of the ways in which stars are fragmented.

1 of 2 pages

# 3 Gwyneth Paltrow

While Stacey focused her analysis upon audiences' memories of stars, the following notes explore how the key points from her theories on spectatorship can be used in the analysis of contemporary stars, and how, in addition to audience research, you can explore issues of spectatorship through a textual analysis of the representation of the star within their films and in newspapers, magazines and web pages. The intention is to provide a solid theoretical framework that could then be applied to the study of any star/spectator relations. While some of the issues within Stacey's work are specific to the historical moment – eg the wartime rationing – you can still encourage students to explore the representation of stars, their appeal and how spectators are encouraged to identify and attempt to copy them.

## *Overview*

Gwyneth Paltrow is ideal as an intertextual case study of female stars because her image is ever changing yet recognisable. She appears to be an image of naturalness, devoid of the artificial construction of the rags-to-riches Cinderella tales of Hollywood. She embodies the ideological ideals of the WASP (White Anglo-Saxon Protestant) American woman. Although sexualised, her sexuality is not so overt that she becomes threatening. She is upper middle class and perpetuates the American dream of success. With hard work and determination, she 'made it' – with a little help from her family contacts.

As a young, white, tall, thin, leggy blonde, she conforms to ideals of Hollywood beauty, but unlike many Hollywood stars, such as Cameron Diaz, she is unlikely to be found on the front cover of a lad's mag such as *FHM* or *Loaded* in her underwear, as 'this month's most sexy' woman. In photographs, she is nearly always represented fully clothed, with a focus on her face and neck. Through the processes of representation, she is constructed as an image, but she is nearly always represented as though this is a naturalised image. Hair flowing, minimal make-up, beaming smile, casual clothes make her more like the 'girl next door', than the aloof superstar. Paltrow as a star text articulates discourses of 'fashion' as a way of life to the female spectator. Her interests are not only in fashion (clothing and hair), but encompass 'lifestyle', including family, relationships, career, home, fitness, diet and spirituality.

As a fashion icon, she echoes and embodies the contents pages of the women's magazines in which she is featured. Rather than a distanced style icon to be worshipped and envied, she exists as a barometer of fashionable and accessible lifestyle trends which can be copied by the female spectator. Fashion for Paltrow (and in turn the female spectator) becomes a means of reinventing the self, in the continual search for a stable and whole self-image, removed from wider contemporary social and cultural concerns.

Like J Lo, Victoria Beckham and Sarah Jessica Parker, Paltrow is featured in a vast range of magazines such as *Glamour*, *Heat*, *Now*, *New Woman*, *Elle* and *Vogue* as a woman that other women should aspire to identify with and copy.

Jackie Stacey's framework can be used as a means of analysing Paltrow both in and outside her films.

### *Escapism*

- **American stars**

Many of the stars that students will encounter and 'like' are American stars from television and/or film. Before moving on to an analysis of Paltrow as a star text, encourage students to discuss more generally the pleasures of American stars. See **Worksheet 18**.

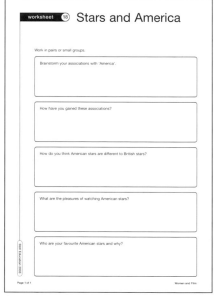

1 page

- **The path to success**

Within magazine and newspaper articles, Gwyneth Paltrow is represented in terms of her difference as an American star – this is tied to representations of class and background. While Jennifer Lopez has reinvented herself as 'J Lo', declaring in her music that, despite all her newfound wealth, she is still 'Jenni from the Block', Gwyneth Paltrow is represented by the media in terms of her background, of upper-middle class refinement. With the 1996 release of *Emma*, Paltrow was hailed as an 'It Girl'. Articles focus upon her background including her education at New York's elite Spence School, her 'Hollywood family' of writer and director father (Bruce Paltrow), stage actress mother (Blythe Danner), and family friends, Steven Spielberg and Michael Douglas.

There is a confidence in the story of her success, which one can argue comes from her family upbringing; from the age of five, Paltrow apparently knew that one day she would be a star:

> 'I've known my whole life that this was going to happen to me in some way [...] You don't think that it really will, but then when it happens you're like 'I knew it would happen'. I believe if you ask any famous person they will have known that they were going to be famous. It's like a predestined thing.' (Shnaynerson 2000: 139)

Gwyneth Paltrow as Emma.

Nevertheless, she is eager to prove that her rise to stardom was due to hard work. She relates having to go through 'a dreary period of losing out, role after role to the same handful of better known actresses' (ibid: 189). See **Worksheet 19** – discussion work on the ideological importance of 'hard work'.

Even so, Paltrow has had a series of 'lucky breaks', assisted by family connections and powerful players willing to help her, from being asked by Steven Spielberg to play the role of Wendy in *Hook*, to becoming Harvey Weinstein's 'Miramax darling'.

**worksheet 19  Stars and hard work**

Why is 'hard work' so important in narratives of a star's success?
Working in pairs or small groups, discuss and make notes on the following:

Why is it seen as important, in our culture, that everyone can make it if only they work hard enough?

Do you believe success is predestined or due to hard work – or a mixture of both?

Identify stars/celebrities whose success was (allegedly) due to:
- Hard work
- Background
- Being discovered

Page 1 of 1                                          Women and Film

1 page

## ● The lure of New York

Manhattan (New York) is integral to the narrative of Paltrow's rise to stardom as a place of opportunity. Paltrow moved from her hometown to the Big Apple in order to grow up and to 'make it'. She remains based in Manhattan and one could argue that with the success in the UK of American programmes such as *Friends* and *Sex and the City*, living in Manhattan has become a signifier of material and personal success. Marriage, children and suburbia as goals for the upwardly mobile twenty-something woman are replaced with the desire to be single and sexually active, have lots of close friends, and live a lifestyle dominated by coffee shops, bars, clubs, designer shops and large, trendy apartments. Thus Paltrow becomes part of this idealised lifestyle, which is far removed from the realities of the isolation, crippling rent, student debts, endless commuting and long working hours of many twenty-something British female spectators. Through our intertextual knowledge, the very mention of 'New York' within an article about Paltrow instantly becomes loaded with connotations of glamour and affluence.

Manhattan provides an escape from the 'drabness of life in Britain' in a manner that echoes Jackie Stacey's discussion of the appeal of Hollywood films for women in the 1940s (Stacey 1994: 109). However, with the reduced cost of air travel and the rapid growth in internet usage, America no longer retains the sense of 'otherworldliness' for spectators as it did for the women in Stacey's study. Not only is American culture now part of our everyday life, but also America is increasingly accessible for British people.

See **Worksheet 20** – stars and cities.

1 page

### Multiple images of the star

The opening scenes of a film are crucial in setting the scene, establishing characters and introducing elements/characters that will prove to be central to the narrative of the text. Therefore, when studying film with students, it is worth spending time analysing the opening scenes of several different films, in order to analyse how meaning is constructed and narratives function.

Doing this helps students to gather case study evidence of the differing ways in which a star is represented within films. It also helps them to develop their skills in textual analysis of 'unseen' texts and research how narratives function to gain and hold the attention of the audience.

● **Textual example 1: *A Perfect Murder***

*A Perfect Murder* (1998) blurs the boundaries between the image of the star and the character. Paltrow is represented as the Upper East Side New York society girl, an image perpetuated extratextually in the representation of Paltrow in magazines such as *Vanity Fair* as an 'It Girl'.

**Worksheet 21** provides questions to support the analysis of the opening scenes of *A Perfect Murder.*

1 page

While Gwyneth Paltrow is an American star, she is sometimes mistaken for British, because of her roles in films such as *Emma* (1996), *Sliding Doors* (1998) and *Shakespeare in Love* (1998). Therefore, while she articulates the otherness of the American star, she also becomes accessible and constructs an illusion of ordinariness through her masquerade of national identity.

● **Textual example 2: *Sliding Doors***

*Sliding Doors* provides an interesting and accessible case study for students, not only in terms of the representation of Paltrow, but also in its narrative techniques. Although it is a mainstream and accessible text (one which many students are likely to have seen due to its screenings on television and availability on video/DVD), it uses many complex narrative techniques in order to tell a multi-strand, parallel narrative. To maximise its usefulness for students, it would be worth screening the whole film, rather than showing clips.

The film centres upon the notion of 'what if'. After being fired from her PR job, Helen (Paltrow) catches/misses the tube, starting a split in the narrative, which follows the Helen who catches the tube as she returns home to find her partner in bed with another woman, and the Helen who misses the tube and continues her relationship with her partner. The narrative shows both sides of the story, at points intertwining and merging through events, characters and places.

While *A Perfect Murder* constructs Paltrow as the Upper East Side New Yorker, in an image that blurs star with character, *Sliding Doors* is set in London with Paltrow playing an English woman from the Home Counties. The film is interesting to analyse because it represents not only different images of Paltrow, but also multiple images of femininity, which provide dichotomies of good versus bad woman and enable multiple points of identification for the female spectator:

| | | |
|---|---|---|
| Helen | As career woman | Fired from her PR job |
| Child | Disruption | Causes the split in the narrative at the tube station |
| Helen | As victim | Being mugged and needing to be rescued |
| Helen | As victim of adultery | When Helen discovers her boyfriend in bed with Lydia |
| Lydia | The 'bad' other woman | Coded as 'other' visually, through brunette hair, as object of the gaze (black underwear and hold-ups), as American. |
| Anna | The best friend | Supports Helen |
| New Helen | Independent woman | Moves on from adultery, to set up own PR company and fall in love with James |
| Old Helen | Girlfriend | Loses PR job and ends up as waitress and sandwich delivery girl |
| Claudia | The other woman | James's estranged wife |

● **Clip 0.00–02.30 – Use of setting and national identity**
Screen the opening sequence of the film and encourage students to make notes based on the questions in **Worksheet 22**.

---

**worksheet** ㉒ **Analysing opening scenes 2: *Sliding Doors***

(US/UK, 1998, Peter Howitt)

Before watching this scene from *Sliding Doors*, read the questions below. When watching the clip, make notes in response to the questions. These will form the basis of class discussion and analysis.

| Clip 0.00–02.30 | |
|---|---|
| What does the bridge in the opening shot connote? | |
| Where is the film set? What visual icons are used to signify setting? | |
| How is Gwyneth Paltrow's character, Helen represented? What can we read about her life based upon setting, costume, and performance? | |
| What impact does the casting of Gwyneth Paltrow in the role of Helen have upon our reading of the text? Why do you think that Paltrow was cast in the role? | |
| To what extent is this the image of Paltrow that we expect? How is it different? What trademarks are missing? | |
| What is the national identity of Paltrow's character in the film? How do we know? | |
| How does our intertextual knowledge of Paltrow the star, impact upon our reading of Paltrow's character of Helen in terms of national identity? | |

Page 1 of 1                                        Women and Film

1 page

The text is rich ground for analysis, especially in terms of its narrative techniques and its representation of London and Britishness and the dichotomies between the characters (especially Helen, Lydia, Gerry and James). As a text to form part of a star study of Paltrow, it is the elements of identification and consumption that are especially useful points for analysis. It is important when undertaking a star study for students to understand the meaning that a star brings to a film. While *Sliding Doors* centres upon a parallel narrative about Helen, the casting of Gwyneth Paltrow in the role brings an additional level of meaning.

Paltrow is constructed within the text as English, yet the representation is one of distance, and in turn escapism, rather than familiarity for many spectators. The film is set in London, but it is a middle-class, white image of England, in which characters love *Monty Python*, go rowing at the weekend and have large apartments in desirable Georgian town houses. It is highly unlikely that a couple with the income of Helen and Gerry could afford such an apartment in London. In addition, cultural diversity is limited to characters that are Scottish, Irish and American.

● **Clip 25.48 – 26.48: Transformation of self**

The first image of Helen (with long, mousy hair) conflicts with our expectations of the image of Paltrow the star. Such a representation can be seen to function in order to enable the Cinderella-like transformation of the star within the film. Thus Helen and in turn Paltrow, in order to move on from her failed relationship and become independent and successful, must transform the image of the self.

Anna as the best friend gives voice to shared knowledge of femininity: 'What you need is a change of image.' The two women use a woman's magazine as inspiration for Helen/Paltrow to copy (with images that bear a striking resemblance to fashion shoots featuring Paltrow). Rather than using the women's magazine as inspiration for clothes to buy, they appropriate the text for their own uses, as inspiration for hairstyles. Anna then provides instruction on how to achieve the look, and the two manipulate their hair, pulling it upwards in order to become closer to the image in the magazine. This process of shared knowledge, pretending and resembling enables Helen/Paltrow to begin her transformation of the self, and it in turn encourages the spectator to identify with the characters.

As the scene progresses, we are also shown the 'other' Helen, who, still with Gerry, is now having to seek work in the traditionally feminine role of waitress and sandwich delivery person. After losing her PR job, she is no longer using the services of the bar and sandwich shop (that were featured earlier in the film), but is the provider. With her long, mousy hair tied back into low plaits while working, Paltrow is far removed from the glamorous image of the star and looks very ordinary. Her ordinariness brings her closer as a point of identification to the spectator, but she does not exist as a point of desire. The other Helen/ Paltrow has the same ordinariness, but is about to embark on the process of transformation.

In the scenes at the hairdresser, the spectator is positioned with Anna, looking on while Helen/Paltrow submits herself to the stylist. She is represented as a fragmented image of woman, shown in a series of close-ups that represent the processes of construction and the work of femininity. Through the lengthy process of cutting, colouring and blow-drying, a new image of Helen/Paltrow is constructed, and narrative time is compressed as Anna is shown becoming increasingly tired of waiting. Finally the new glamorous image of Helen/Paltrow is revealed to Anna and the spectator, as the hairdresser spins her around to reveal Helen's new short blonde hair.

Gwyneth Paltrow and John Hannah in *Sliding Doors*.

The new Helen (Gwyneth Paltrow) in *Sliding Doors*.

The image of Helen/Paltrow that is revealed is closer to the image of Paltrow the star with which we are familiar. Thus the constructed image of Paltrow appears more 'natural' than the image of Helen with the long, mousy hair.

### The intertextuality of Paltrow

The familiarity of the image of Paltrow as the 'new' Helen in *Sliding Doors* is the result of the intertextuality of Paltrow as a fashion icon. In *Sliding Doors*, when Helen has her hair cut, the scene becomes filled with additional meaning – not only does the character reveal a different image of self, but so, too, does Gwyneth Paltrow. We bring our intertextual knowledge of the star to our reading of the scene, largely because:

- The star is represented through the publicity images (often stills from the film) and intertextually through television, newspapers, magazines, and website interviews that promote the film. This is combined with the use of personal appearances at premieres, award ceremonies etc.
- Many magazines and newspaper articles about films and stars are taken from press kits and other sources, combined with stock images of the star. Many articles include quotes from and photos of the star from the press kit, not from personal interviews or photo sessions. Images are often used without being anchored in terms of the actual date or location where the photo was taken, and instead the captions are used to support the comments made in the article.

- Multiple images exist of the star at any given moment – we are never quite sure what they really look like 'now'.
- The photographs section of www.gwynethpaltrow.org is useful for a range of images of Paltrow.

With each new film or premiere, Paltrow reveals a different image of self. From the matching his and hers haircuts when she was Brad Pitt's girlfriend, to flowing blonde locks, to her dyed brown hair for her role in *Bounce* (2000). Countless column inches are dedicated to Gwyneth's new look in magazines such as *New Woman*, *Woman's Journal*, *Heat*, *Now*, where women are encouraged to 'look like Gwyneth for just £6.99'. Through multiple images of self, she presents multiple points of identification for the spectator to attempt to copy.

### Paltrow the fashion icon

In addition to her hair, Paltrow's wardrobe in *Sliding Doors* is loaded with intertextual meaning. As the new Helen, her wardrobe undertakes a subtle shift and becomes somewhat more sensual and glamorous, while retaining a casual, androgynous look, supplied by Calvin Klein. There has been a shift away from 'costume design' within contemporary cinema to the integration of fashion in films set in the present (and in some cases also the past and future). Fashion in a film enables both a promotion of the designer and a continual blurring of character and star.

While Helen's/Paltrow's clothes are not spectacular, they stand out within the narrative as exclusive and classic. The use of luxurious fabrics, especially the soft, fitted cashmere jumpers, connote sexuality through their pared-down ease and lack of superficial detail. Most notably they create a 'look', which works to articulate the construction of character and interacts with the image of Gwyneth Paltrow, the star outside the text.

- In the 1990s, Paltrow, according to Vogue editor Anna Wintour, became well known as the actress that every designer wanted to dress (Katz 1996: 2), most notably Calvin Klein.
- During Paltrow's rise to success, Calvin Klein was reported to have sent outfits for her to wear to premieres and asked her to model on the catwalk and in print campaigns.
- Paltrow, through the combination of her looks and background, brings connotations of androgyny, naturalness and Americanness to the Calvin Klein brand. By wearing the clothes, she covertly endorses the label in a more subtle and seemingly natural manner, embodying the Calvin Klein 'lifestyle', rather than just modelling the clothes.

Paltrow could pass as a model, yet she retains an air of ordinariness. Unlike Catherine Zeta Jones, or Jennifer Lopez, she is very rarely shown highly made up, in glamorous clothes that reveal her flesh. The key image of Paltrow attempting glamour and refinement and 'getting it wrong' was the pink Ralph Lauren gown she wore when she accepted her Oscar for *Shakespeare in Love*, which was too big for her. She is not so much a style icon (like Sarah Jessica Parker's character Carrie in *Sex and the City*), as a fashion icon. Her personal style is made up of a bricolage of designer labels that signify her success. Paltrow has said: 'I'd be happy to wear a cashmere tank, a pair of jeans, cargo pants or khakis every day. I always pack Turnbull & Asser men's pyjamas, leather pants and a big, soft sweater. I never wear one person's clothes head to toe. Right now I'm wearing my favourite T by Mark Jacobs. The jeans are Diesel. My boots are D&G, the coat is Armani. Mixing the elements is what personal style is all about.' (Paltrow in Rubenstein 1999) Paltrow's style therefore is not associated with a specific 'look' or specific garments (unlike say Liz Hurley, Jennifer Lopez), but with brands.

## ● **Tips for teaching**

● Paltrow is not the only star to be associated with fashion brands. Ask students to gather, analyse and discuss examples of how stars are overtly and covertly used to promote fashion and beauty brands. See **Worksheet 23** on stars and designers.

● *Glamour* magazine is very useful for students to use in compiling case study material on stars and fashion (and representation, genre and advertising), and it is cheaper and smaller than *Vogue*, *Elle* and *Marie Claire*, so students – especially male students – are willing to buy it and bring it into lessons, saving you a fortune in colour photocopying and providing material for their case studies.

1 of 2 pages

### The work of femininity and consumption

Women's magazines provide multiple pleasures for not only the female, but also the male spectator.

● Get students to discuss their consumption of women's magazines and the pleasures they offer (**Worksheet 24**).

One of the key pleasures of magazines is the notion of shared knowledge, getting closer to the star by gaining 'exclusive' information about the products that they consume, the diets and exercise regimes they follow and the clothes they wear. Central to achieving beauty and success according to the rules of the woman's magazine is:

● The work of femininity
● Consumption.

While no mention is made of Paltrow having to lose weight to become a star (compare with Jennifer Aniston, for example), Paltrow's 'naturally' thin body is attributed to ashtanga yoga. Yoga has become the 'new gym' and a lifestyle trend requiring immense dedication. It can be done at home and has the potential to be beneficial to both body and mind.

1 of 2 pages

● Ask students to identify which stars are following this trend.
● Explore issues of spirituality and the rise in 'alternative' religions and discuss why there would be such a concern for exercise to fulfil a spiritual function as well as a physical one.

Potentially we can all do yoga, but few of us have the time, inclination or determination to follow it with the dedication it requires to be effective. While we can attempt to copy the stars, become more like them, we never quite succeed.

### Ideas for development work on stars, representation and audience pleasures

● Encourage students to analyse fan sites. How are the stars represented? What pleasures are offered?

- Which stars are audiences encouraged to copy? Develop intertextual case studies, with material from magazines, newspapers and websites. Stars featured in advertisements for clothing and beauty products, and articles on how to copy stars provide excellent case study material and are also useful for advertising and marketing questions.
- Develop case studies on films that have influenced fashion and had tie-ins with clothing and beauty companies, eg *Die Another Day* (2002), *The Matrix* (1999) and *The Matrix Reloaded* (2003).

# CASE STUDY 3:
# Genre, representation and media language

The purpose of this case study is to provide a framework for using the Heritage/Post-heritage genre as a means of exploring how a genre has changed and evolved to become increasingly self-aware and self-referential in the pleasures that it offers to the spectator.

## 1 The Heritage film – theoretical framework

If students are given a choice over what genres they study during their course, they will tend to pick those that they like and already consume, most notably situation comedy, soap opera and horror. They may have specific texts that they wish to study, eg *The X-Files* or *Buffy the Vampire Slayer.* Studying texts in class or for coursework that students like and already consume does have its advantages – they have knowledge about the text and can engage with it. They are also more likely to be enthusiastic (at least initially) about studying the text.

But there are also disadvantages – students become upset when you 'spoil' their favourite film or programme, when they can no longer 'just watch it' and not pull it to pieces. Also students may find it difficult to move beyond descriptive, fan-based essays and to produce critical evaluations of texts, resulting in a 'common sense' approach to the genre. If you pick a genre that they do not usually watch, they have to work harder to engage with the debates and texts, and may find themselves surprised that they actually enjoy doing this.

### Studying the Heritage/Post-heritage genre as part of 'women and film'
For many students, the study of a 'costume'-based drama will instantly place them at a critical distance from the text, as it is not a genre that many of them will go out of their way to consume. Central to the study of the Heritage/Post-heritage film in terms of women and film will be a focus upon representation and *mise en scène* analysis through exploring:

- The pleasures of costume
- Costume and identity.

'Costume dramas' tend to be perceived as a 'woman's genre' and an 'old people's' genre. The genre, though, is changing and becoming increasingly self-aware, self-referential and multi-generic. Films such as *Shakespeare in Love* (1998), *Plunkett and Macleane* (1999), *Moulin Rouge* (2001) and *Gangs of New York* (2002) do not promote themselves as costume-based dramas, but films set in the past that have relevance to a contemporary audience.

Before studying Heritage and Post-heritage films in depth, you will need to encourage students to explore the problems of genre definition. Costume drama, Heritage film, historical drama and literary adaptation are terms often used interchangeably to describe films set in the past. **Worksheet 25** encourages students to discuss their understanding of historical genres, nostalgia and at what point the past becomes 'history'.

In attempting to discuss and analyse films set in the past, one is instantly drawn into a complex set of debates in which the 'correct' generic term for classifying a text is unclear. Not only are the texts themselves increasingly changing and evolving, but also they have, since the mid-1980s, become not only popular, but also seen to be 'worthy' of academic critical attention.

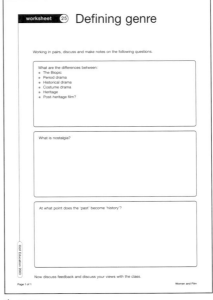

1 page

### *Defining the Heritage film*

In the mid-1980s, a collection of films sharing a number of recognisable characteristics emerged that retrospectively have been termed 'Heritage' films. These films are often associated with Merchant Ivory's literary adaptations such as *A Room with a View* (1986) and *Howards End* (1992).

Heritage cinema, though, refers to a range of texts (including British television adaptations) often based upon 'popular classics' by 'Forster, Austen, Shakespeare, Balzac, Dumas, Hugo, Zola' (Hill 1999: xvi). The most quoted/analysed examples of Heritage cinema are:

- *A Room with a View*
- *Chariots of Fire* (1981)
- *Maurice* (1987)
- *Shadowlands* (1993)
- *Howards End.*

As John Hill notes, during the 1980s, E M Forster's work proved the most popular and five films were based upon his books (*A Passage to India* (1984), *A Room with a View*, *Maurice*, *Where Angels Fear to Tread* (1991) and *Howards End*) (Hill 1999: 78, Hutchings 1995: 213).

### Key theorists

Andrew Higson (1993, 1996), Tana Wollen (1991) and Cairns Craig (1991) have each worked towards classifying, categorising and theorising the 'key formal, thematic, iconographic and industrial characteristics' (Higson 1996:232) of Heritage films and television screen fictions of the 1980s and 1990s. They have made some of the boundaries a little clearer, not only in terms of defining what constitutes a Heritage film, but also their differences from other costume-based subgenres.

Beyond defining characteristics and tendencies, their work, together with that of Claire Monk, Richard Dyer and Peter Hutchings (in the United Kingdom), has focused primarily upon the films as examples of British national cinema. They have also focused on the texts' thematic concerns of class, politics, nostalgic cultural tourism, and (to a much lesser extent) issues of gender and sexuality.

### Key characteristics of the Heritage film

Andrew Higson's work on the Heritage film provides a useful starting point for attempting to define the 'key formal, thematic, iconographic and industrial characteristics of the Heritage films of the 1980s and 1990s' (Higson 1996: 232).

- At www.bfi.org.uk/tfms, you will find a summary of the **key characteristics of the Heritage film** adapted from Higson's work. The summary can be printed off and used as a handout / revision sheet with students, and also act as a framework for analysis.

### Analysis of the trailer for A Room with a View

Using trailers is an ideal way of very quickly gaining an understanding of the key characteristics of a text and how it adheres to and/or challenges generic conventions. Use **Worksheet 26** to guide your students through analysis of this particular example from *A Room with a View*.

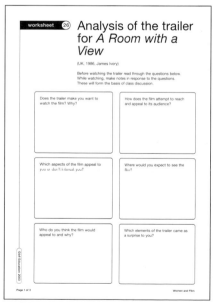

1 of 3 pages

DVD releases of films increasingly include original theatrical trailers as a bonus feature. These are incredibly useful with students, not only to further their knowledge of the text itself, but also:

- To develop their skills in analysing 'unseen' texts;
- As part of gathering case study material on the ways in which films are promoted as part of studying advertising and marketing;
- To develop their understanding of how texts gain and hold the attention of their audience.

Analysing trailers also enables you to develop students' skills in comparative critical analysis, as within a single session you can study a number of different trailers. The DVD release of *A Room with a View* includes the original theatrical trailer (available online from www.play.com).

The trailer presents the audience with a tale of romance set against the Italian landscape, with beautiful period costumes and interior design. The pace of the trailer, like the film, is slow and episodic. It focuses upon a female-centred narrative of characters, emotion and 'talk', rather than goal-orientated action, explosions and violence.

Initially you should screen the whole trailer once, and let the students just watch it. Before working through it in detail, have them discuss their reactions to it. Do not be put off if they say that they think it looks boring. Try to explore and develop any differing viewpoints – especially based on gender. When I have undertaken this task with students, the female students seem far more interested in the film than the males. Use this as a springboard to discussing gendered pleasures.

### The past as a means of working through the concerns of the present

Heritage films can be seen to represent a nostalgic, conservative image of the national past. As Colin McArthur argues, 'No matter what period history writing or historical drama is ostensibly dealing with, in reality it is providing for the ideological needs of the present.' (McArthur 1981: 288)

The work of the Heritage critic does not focus on whether the films are accurate representations of 'history', but rather on how the thematic concerns of the text and their nostalgic vision of the past provide an escape from present issues such as multicultural and multiracial tensions, unemployment and inequalities in income and living standards.

## 2 Re-reading the Heritage film – the pleasures of Heritage

Academic work on Heritage films has tended to concentrate on the ways in which the films promoted the Heritage industry and cultural tourism, and articulated conservative nostalgic visions of the national past. Critics have expressed surprise and guilty pleasure at any level of enjoyment of the films.

### The absence of costume

Despite the use of historical costuming in the Heritage film, there is virtually no mention by the Heritage critics of how costume functions to support character construction or its potential for pleasure. This (as my own research explores) is somewhat strange – surely one of the pleasures of the costume film is the escapism provided through the difference of the costumes from contemporary fashion?

In her book *Undressing Cinema: Costume and Identity in the Movies* (1997), Stella Bruzzi argues that Heritage films such as *Howards End* and *Sense and Sensibility* (1995) 'look through rather than at costume' (Bruzzi 1997: 36). This goes some way perhaps to explaining the absence of costume analysis within critical theory on the Heritage film. In films that look 'through' clothing, 'the focus of the costume design is to signal their historical accuracy' (Bruzzi 1997: 36). In films that look 'at' clothing, costume functions to create 'an alternative discourse' and one that often overrides the dominant narrative. In turn the eroticism of the clothes is highlighted (Bruzzi 1997: 36).

Therefore, in a film such as *A Room with a View*, costume functions in order to signify that the film is set in the past and to enhance its position as a 'quality' film through the attention to detail of the costuming. It does not draw attention to itself as the site of erotic tension. Indeed, the use of costume, with the tight, high necks of the women's blouses, can highlight their sexual repression within the narrative.

Heritage films can be re-read in terms of the pleasures they offer as 'costume' films. There are two key elements to this pleasure – escapism and landscape.

### Costume and escapism

One of the central pleasures of costume-based dramas is the way in which they enable the spectator to be transported into the past and away from the day-to-day realities of their lives. Key to such escapism is the visualisation of the past through *mise en scène*. Higson *et al* discuss the use of a 'museum aesthetic' in the Heritage film, in the ways the camera functions to enable the spectator to survey the historical spectacle of the interiors. The camera lingers in mid- and long shots, through slow-paced editing and long takes, to enable us to look at the lavish antiques. Characters move slowly around rooms, touching objects; details are reflected in large, gilt mirrors. In turn, a visual narrative is created that enables us to consume the visual splendour of the past usually only seen in magazines or behind the ropes of National Trust properties. (See for example: Lucy playing piano and talking to Mr Bebe, 11.37–13.00)

While Higson *et al* acknowledge such visual pleasures, the use of costume is also central to the scenes. The film enables us to survey the fashions of the Edwardian era. Instead of the lifelessness of the museum aesthetic of the costume on a mannequin in a display case, we can see in close-up the details of the fabric and embroidery, and see how the clothes move when they are worn. Woman in these scenes becomes part of the decorative surface to be consumed. The viewer is drawn to the details, and the otherness of the costume. Its appeal is in its difference from contemporary clothing – the size of the waist, the high necklines, the noise of the fabric, the attention to detail in the embroidery.

Central to the pleasure of such clothes is not only looking at them, but also, as Richard Dyer argues, imagining yourself 'touching or wearing them' (2000: 46). The audience may not want to be the characters, but they may want to imagine what it would be like if they were. If costume were not important in these scenes, imagine how different they would be if the characters were wearing contemporary fashions. If Lucy wore a Kappa tracksuit and the Reverend Bebe wore a football shirt, would the scene carry the same meaning or pleasures?

### Costume and landscape

In the interior scenes of *A Room with a View,* costume signifies historical accuracy, repression and the construction and performance of class identity. However, characters are not restricted to interior scenes, and the film uses the exterior scenes to enable the emancipation of the female characters.

In costume-based dramas, the countryside enables escapist pleasures and creates spaces where, as Sue Harper argues, 'only feelings reside' (1994). The countryside and the woodland lake in *A Room with a View* enable the characters to be free from social conventions and explore their sexuality. Higson *et al* emphasise the use of the 'touristic gaze' and picture-postcard imagery, yet the exterior scenes are more visually stunning because of the figures travelling through the landscapes.

The landscape scenes offer visual pleasures of:

- The movement of clothing – skirt billowing, coats flapping etc;
- The inappropriateness of clothing to landscape – the fetishistic pleasures of skirts being hoisted up while one moves through the landscape;
- The potential for the countryside to enable spaces in which the clothes can be shed.

### Key scenes:
- Charlotte and Miss Lavish: Clip 13.25–14.05
- The cornfield – Lucy and George kiss: Clip 33.25–35.25
- The bathing scene– stripping off and male homoeroticism: Clip 1hr 00.27–1hr 04: 42

### *The pleasures of the male*

An integral element of the pleasures of costume within the Heritage film can be seen to be the representation of 'unthreatening' males. The male within the Heritage film is represented, one can argue, for the female/non-masculine spectator. Rather than leading the narrative action, he is feminised and presented as the object of the gaze.

The use of historical setting allows, as Richard Dyer argues, for a very specific pleasure, that of 'looking at nice men, wearing nice clothes' (Dyer 2000: 46). Watching 'good-looking men, well turned out in retro clothes amid period objects' (Dyer 2000: 43) offers a level of visual pleasure disallowed within much of mainstream narrative cinema. Heritage enables an escape from the shaven-headed, football shirt-wearing image of contemporary masculinity to a softer image.

As Claire Monk has argued, *A Room with a View* offers the rare pleasure of 'active straight female looking' (Monk 1997: 1 part 2). Through the eyes of Lucy, the spectator is given the opportunity to gaze at the male (most notably the naked homoerotic male – and in a PG film!)

## 3 Post-heritage – costume and identity

The 1990s saw a significant period of development and change in the visual style, thematic concerns and pleasures offered to spectators of costume-based dramas. One can argue that the most significant shift was towards an overt focus upon the ways in which costume functions in the construction and performance of gendered identity. No longer was costume looked through, now it was being looked at. The simmering pleasures of the Heritage film were made explicit and central to the thematic concerns of the narrative.

Claire Monk, in her article 'Sexuality and the Heritage' (*Sight and Sound*, 1995), argued that Heritage films with their increased focus upon 'feminine, queer and ambiguous sexualities' were changing and shifting to what she termed an era of 'Post-heritage' films, such as:

- *The Piano* (1993)
- *Orlando* (1992)
- *Tom and Viv* (1994)
- *Carrington* (1995)
- *The Age of Innocence* (1993).

These films, according to Monk, 'revel in the visual pleasures of Heritage', yet also seem to distance themselves. Their concern is not with constructing a nostalgic vision of the past, but with using the past as a safe place in which to explore narratives of gender and sexuality.

### Jane Campion's The Piano

Films such as Jane Campion's *The Piano* (1993) proved that 'feminist/women's cinema' could utilise the conventions of mainstream narrative cinema to construct a feminine/feminist discourse that explores issues of subjectivity, history, gender, sexuality and desire. The film achieved international mainstream success 'attracting large audiences and creating genuine art' (Quart 1994: 54), with Campion remaining 'in control of the creative vision and production' (see O'Regan 1995). Between Campion, the cast and crew, the film won more than 20 awards, was nominated for more than ten more and Campion was, in 1994, the first woman to win the Best Director award at the Cannes Film Festival (Quart 1994: 54). (Arguably the winning of awards can be seen as achieving institutional 'success' within mainstream cinema, especially the Oscars. Whether the filmmakers, cast and crew themselves value the awards is a different matter.)

The film, despite being grounded in an auteur-based cinema, proved popular not only with audiences beyond the regional film theatres, but also within both journalistic and academic discourses. It has become an example of women's/feminist cinema that is 'legitimate' as a text to discuss and led to a surge of critical theory and surprised confessions by critics of being 'moved by the clothes' (Bruzzi 1997: xiii).

### Post-heritage in the mainstream

Films such as *The Piano*, *Tom and Viv*, *Carrington*, *and Orlando* can be termed Post-heritage, and achieved a level of box-office and critical success (especially *The Piano*), but one can argue that they were not specifically marketed for a mainstream audience. With the release of films such as *Titanic* (1997), *William Shakespeare's Romeo and Juliet* (1996), *Shakespeare in Love* (1998) and *Elizabeth* (1998) during the latter half of the 1990s, there was a significant shift of Post-heritage into the mainstream.

One cannot easily apply genre as a theoretical approach to analysing such texts. *Titanic* is not the same type of text as, say, *Elizabeth*. The newer films subvert and play with genre conventions creating multi-generic hybrids.

### Key characteristics of the post-Piano Post-heritage film

At www.bfi.org.uk/tfms you will find a summary of the **key characteristics of the post-*Piano* Post-heritage film**. The summary can be printed off and used as a handout with students and act as a framework for analysis.

### Costume and the construction of gender and sexual identity

These more recent, Post-heritage films are very self-conscious. They provide spectators with the pleasures of Heritage spectacle and have shifted and responded to the critical discourses that surround Heritage in attempting to appeal to a wider audience. They have much in common with the

Gainsborough historical costume melodramas of the 1940s, which contained a 'downplaying of historical accuracy in favour of both spectacle and a focus on the emotional lives of… characters' (Cook 1996: 78).

Films such as *Elizabeth* and *Shakespeare in Love* have an explicit thematic concern with clothing:

- As spectacle – drawing attention to the details, colour, fabric, movement, number of costume changes, the eroticism of costume;
- As a means of constructing and changing identity – not just multiple images of self.

While *The Piano* focused upon essentialist notions of gender, the more recent films have taken the approach of gender and sexuality as performance (tied to the work of Judith Butler). Therefore, through costume and repeated performance, identity becomes fluid.

### Elizabeth

*Elizabeth* (Shekhar Kapur, 1998) has been the subject of academic critical attention as a key text in recent developments in the Post-heritage genre. It subverts the conventions of Heritage, but continues a tradition of 'quality' filmmaking. It takes the past and reworks it from a contemporary perspective, most notably in its representation of Queen Elizabeth. Elizabeth is represented as sexually active – conflicting with the historical perception of her as being a virgin. Then she is transformed and reconstructed, through costume and non-verbal performance, into the role of Virgin Queen.

There are many scenes that could be used with students to illustrate the ways in which costume functions in *Elizabeth*, but the scenes in **Worksheet 27** are potentially some of the most useful (but by no means limit yourself to these).

worksheet 27 **Analysis of *Elizabeth***
(UK, 1998, Shekhar Kapur)

1 of 5 pages

### Shakespeare in Love

John Madden's *Shakespeare in Love* (1998) is a more accessible text than *Elizabeth* for many students, due to its use of stars (it could be tied to a study of Paltrow) and elements of romantic comedy. The two films are often seen as a pair, as they were released at around the same time and competed against one another at the 1999 Academy Awards. Both also featured the casting of a new generation of up-and-coming stars, including Gwyneth Paltrow, Cate Blanchett, Joseph Fiennes and Ben Affleck. As *Elizabeth*, but to a somewhat lesser extent, *Shakespeare in Love* has received academic critical attention.

In its DVD release the film was promoted as:

> 'a romantic comedy for the 1990s set in the 1590s, telling the witty sexy story behind the creation of the greatest love story of them all – *Romeo and Juliet*'.

The film works from its beginning to challenge the audience's expectation of the costume-based drama, especially in its use of:

- Stars – especially young and upcoming stars, combined with the casting of TV stars and classic 'Heritage' actors;
- Camera work – skewed angles, rapid editing, zooming close-ups;
- Comedic elements.

As with *Elizabeth*, however, the film has moments in which it revels in Heritage spectacle through its slow crane shots of exteriors.

*Gender fluidity and masquerade*

The key representation issues in *Shakespeare in Love* of interest are:

- Hyperfemininity
- Cross-dressing
- Gender slippage.

Gwyneth Paltrow, as Viola cross-dressing as Thomas Kent in order to gain access to the stage, refelcts the most obvious use of costume to construct gender identity within the film. Equally, however, Paltrow/Viola constructs her femininity.

Costume therefore is made an explicit thematic focus in the text, as a means of exploring 'feminist' concerns (especially in the work of Judith Butler) about how gender can be seen as 'drag', both constructed through performance, and fluid. Through clothing we can leave behind our gendered self and become someone else.

## ● Tips for teaching

- David Gauntlett's pages on Judith Butler at *www.theory.org.uk/ctr-butl.htm* provide a useful summary of her ideas and a range of further reading and links. Be warned, though – Butler's writing is notorious for being hard reading, so if you are interested in finding out more, start with the secondary sources. Students at this level do not need to read her.
- In analysing representations of gender, it is useful for students to explore to what extent they feel that gender is biologically or culturally constructed. If it is culturally constructed through repetition and ritual, then it has the potential to be changed.

## ● Hyperfemininity in *Shakespeare in Love*

As an image of femininity, Viola (Paltrow) exists as property. She belongs to her father, who attempts to sell her to Lord Wessex in return for rubies and land, with a promise that if she does not 'breed' Wessex can send her back. Viola is represented as having no voice in her destiny as a woman. In performing her feminine role, she constructs herself as an idealised image of femininity. The spectator is given privileged knowledge of this process of construction as we see Viola prepare to attend the ball.

worksheet **28** Analysis of femininity in *Shakespeare in Love*

(US/UK, 1998, John Madden)

- See **Clip 25.05–29.17.** Viola preparing to attend the ball, and **Worksheet 28** for scene analysis questions.

1 page

## ● Cross-dressing in *Shakespeare in Love*

The use of cross-dressing in the film is in a sense historically accurate in relation to Elizabethan theatre. Cross-dressing and impersonations of gender were an important theme in the sixteenth and seventeenth centuries, in which theatre became a space to emphasise that 'gender differences were more flexible than they appeared' (Bullough and Bullough 1993: 74). In this period, though, it was men who cross-dressed as women, as women were not allowed to perform on stage. When men performed femininity, their masculinity was ever present. Therefore in having a woman cross-dress as a man to achieve her goals, the film is not historically accurate. Instead it uses the past as a safe place in which to construct a subtle 'feminist' narrative about women's roles and opportunities. To achieve her objective of working on the stage, Viola must 'pass' as a man.

● See **Clip 21.06–22.25** where Viola auditions while passing as Thomas Kent, and **Worksheet 29** for scene analysis questions.

● **Gender slippage in Shakespeare in Love**

Judith Butler suggests that 'passing' – ie the most successful drag, when you can't tell the 'real' identity – is the ultimate gender subversion. BUT if the drag is so good that you can't tell, then how do you know that subversion is taking place at all? In order to see the processes of drag and passing, you also need to see the 'real', 'natural' sexed body underneath. Therefore, when Viola is in the private sphere of her bedroom, we are allowed to see not only the work of femininity, but also the ways in which she constructs/deconstructs masculinity by binding her body and wearing the wig and moustache.

● See **Clip: 40.40–46.15** – Will and Thomas's/Viola's first kiss and **Worksheet 30** for scene analysis questions.

The text raises issues of homo-eroticism through Will's desire for Thomas, but this desire is suppressed and made safe by Will's discovery that Thomas is actually Viola:

● Before the two can make love, Viola is made 'safe' by being signalled as feminine through her long blonde hair – her short dark wig suddenly vanishes.

● In the casting of Paltrow – her body is androgynous, rather than overtly curvy – the desirable image of the female body does not highlight bust, hips and waist, but is almost boyish. The camera lingers upon the slenderness of the body, long neck, collar bones.

1 page

1 page

- However, the discovery of the real body of Viola not only heightens desire, but also normalises heterosexuality. The camera lingers upon the body, especially Viola's breasts, to 'prove' that she is 'really' a woman.
- The scene also enables the Thomas/Will kissing scenes later in the film to be made safe, as the spectator knows that Thomas is really a woman.

Within the film there are two key moments of slippage:

- When she forgets to remove the moustache;
- When she sees the mouse – causing her real hair to slip out.
- See **Clip 36.20–38.45** of the meeting with Wessex to arrange to see the Queen (moustache) and **Clip 1hr 21.00–1hr 23.14** performing on the stage, and **Worksheet 31**.

- For further development work, students could explore the use of female drag – male characters dressing as women – and issues of homoeroticism. In the scenes

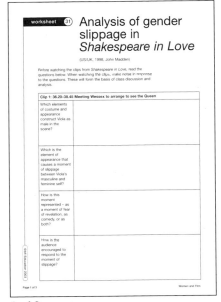

1 of 3 pages

where men dress as women it is easy to see through the drag. The performance is over the top, and the 'real' elements of male identity slip through – facial hair, body shape and movement, voice.

Key scenes:

- Kissing on the stage: Clip 47.44–49.25
- Will masquerading as the nurse: Clip 56.45–1hr 01.42

## 4  Recent developments – moving beyond Post-heritage

During Claire Monk's workshop on Heritage cinema at the British Film Institute's Media Studies Conference (July 2001), she argued that with the release in the 1990s of such films as *The Piano*, *Titanic*, *Elizabeth* and *Shakespeare in Love*, such dramatic changes took place in the visual style and thematic concerns of costume-based films that the existing theoretical debates surrounding Heritage cinema were no longer sufficient to encompass the diverse range of films that had been released. In turn, she argued that, 'we need new debates and new terms to discuss these new films' (2001).

While *Elizabeth* and *Shakespeare in Love* are both very important examples of how Post-heritage has continued to shift since films such as *The Piano*, it is essential to bear in mind this on-going process of evolution and development. Both the terms 'Heritage' and 'Post-heritage' are no longer sufficient to define the range of films that are being released.

In order to attract as wide an audience as possible and increase box-office takings, costume-based dramas are playing to audience expectations and desires, and simultaneously playing with them. These are no longer films aimed at a female spectator, but tend to blur the boundaries between genres in order to produce films that will also appeal to the young male spectator. After *Elizabeth* and *Shakespeare in Love*, Post-heritage is no longer restricted to 'corset films', but increasingly is self-referential, intertextual, playful and ironic in its use of Heritage and Post-heritage spectacle, conventions and themes.

- The recent past has become the focus of what can be termed 'retro/nostalgia' films such as *Chocolat* (2000), *The Talented Mr Ripley* (1999) and *Captain Corelli's Mandolin* (2001). These lovingly construct an image of the past dominated by beautiful stars in beautiful clothes and beautiful settings.
- Genres collide and are played with in ironic, self-referential texts that blur the boundaries of past and present to create spectacular visual narratives in what can be termed 'postmodern Post-heritage' films, eg *Plunkett and Macleane* (1999) and *Moulin Rouge!* (2001).
- The trailers for *Plunkett and Macleane* and *Moulin Rouge!* are particularly useful for illustrating the self-conscious play on Heritage/Post-heritage expectations. The *Plunkett and Macleane* trailer is available on the DVD. The *Moulin Rouge!* trailer is available on the feature-packed double disc DVD and on the website: *www.clubmoulinrouge.com*.

### Gangs of New York

Martin Scorsese's *Gangs of New York* (2002) further complicates any attempt to create new terms and new debates in Post-heritage. Can genre be used as a framework to analyse such a text, or is it more useful to consider it as a 'Scorsese film'?

The film self-consciously disrupts our expectations of films set in the past. Violence is used to excess – this is not 'nice' viewing by any stretch of the imagination. We see the gruesome details of conflict and death – blood spurting, knives and spears graphically penetrating bodies. Realism is taken to such extremes that it becomes theatrical. The audience is given the 'pretty boy' object of the female gaze – Leonardo DiCaprio – and then he is beaten to a pulp. Masculinity is not so pretty now.

Sandy Powell, who designed the costumes for *Shakespeare in Love*, also designed the costumes for *Gangs of New York* which are intrusive in the narrative – they are showy: we notice what characters are wearing. But this, too, is played with. While there are beautiful items of clothing, or parts of a garment are very beautiful, they are teamed with other items that clash and jar. For instance:

- Cameron Diaz's outfit at the 'theatre' when she has knives thrown at her is revealed through a focus in mid-shot that highlights the turquoise colours and kimono-style tailoring and embroidery of the upper half of the dress. This creates a strong image, especially when combined with her long, tousled red hair in tendrils that draw attention to the juxtaposing of fabric and flesh around her neck. The camera then zooms out to reveal a tartan skirt – while both are fabulous showy fabrics, they clash and disrupt the potential for visual pleasures of costume. One suddenly becomes very aware of the look of the costume.
- Daniel Day Lewis's character wears some fabulous coats, and the camera lingers upon them, but his appearance does not give the audience the visual pleasure they may be anticipating. Unlike Johnny Lee Miller in *Plunkett and Macleane*, his historical clothes are teamed not with a modern hairstyle, but with an 'historically accurate' style of long, greasy hair that he repeatedly smoothes down, highlighting just how dirty it is. A large, dark handlebar moustache covers his chiselled looks. By no means is he constructed as a pleasing object of the gaze for the spectator.

- Analysis of the trailer available online at:
  *www.apple.com/trailers/miramax/gangs_of_new_york/*.
- Analysis of the website at: *www.gangsofnewyork.com*.

*Gangs of New York*, while difficult to categorise in terms of generic characteristics, embodies the generic shifts that are taking place. Post-heritage film is increasingly not only moving into the mainstream, but also becoming more self-aware. It is using its pleasures not only to target the female spectator, but also to shed its 'woman's film' identity, by becoming increasingly male-centred in terms of point of view, identification, thematic concerns and visual narratives.

One is left wondering, where does this leave the female spectator? Will all pleasure be diminished? Will she be left once again re-reading, negotiating and searching for the moments of pleasure within the text, or will other genres change to open up alternative spaces for female representation and pleasures?

***Ideas for further work on genre, representation and media language***

- Analysis of other Post-heritage films: *Chocolat*, *The Talented Mr Ripley*, *Captain Corelli's Mandolin*, *Plunkett and Macleane*, *Moulin Rouge*.
- Analysis of films set in the recent past: *Austin Powers* (1997) (and sequels), *The Wedding Singer* (1998), *24 Hour Party People* (2002), or films set in the 'present' with flashbacks – *Spy Game* (2001), *High Fidelity* (2000).
- Analysis of costume in non-historical costume genres. How does costume function in action, science fiction, teen flicks, gangster films, musicals, and comic book adaptations? Identify examples of films in which costume is used to construct identity and/or as showy spectacle.

# Glossary

**Bricolage**
The putting together of different elements, genres and styles in a self-conscious and playful manner.

**Counter cinema**
Film genre which questions and subverts the conventions of mainstream narrative cinema.

**Director**
The person in charge of the creative vision of a film.

**Dominant ideologies**
Those value or belief systems which support the interests of the most powerful groups within societies. Often seen as 'common sense' beliefs.

**Filmmaker**
To begin with, the person who had total control over a film – from the original idea to directing, shooting, and editing. Nowadays most films are the result of the work of a number of people. The director may be the most influential member of the team but other team members such as the producer, the cinematographer and the editor may also influence the final shape of the film.

**Heritage film**
A term applied retrospectively by academic critics, including Andrew Higson (1993, 1996), to categorise a collection of costume-based films released between the mid-1980s and early 1990s. Merchant Ivory's adaptations of E M Forster's novels are good examples.

**Identification**
The processes in which the spectator sympathises or engages with a character.

**Intertextuality**
The process of creating meaning through reference to the audience's knowledge of other media texts.

**Mediation**
The way in which reality is changed through the processes of media production.

### Mise en scène
The combined effect of visual elements within the frame.

### Multigeneric hybrid
A film that combines multiple genres in order to create something new.

### Multi-strand narrative
A text with multiple storylines, often from the point of view of different characters.

### Narrative resolution
Clear closure at the end of a narrative (story).

### Negotiation
The process by which texts can be re-read to find alternative meanings and pleasures that disrupt the dominant reading of the text.

### Object of the gaze
The process by which a person (usually female) becomes sexualised and passive through the 'I' of the camera/central protagonist and, in turn, the audience.

### Persuasive techniques
The ways in which our attention is gained and we are encouraged to buy/consume a product – eg shock tactics, humour, sex, stereotypes, repetition.

### Post-heritage film
A term coined by Claire Monk (1995) to describe a collection of films that emerged in the early 1990s which demonstrated a shift in the heritage film to a more obvious thematic concern with gender and sexual identities.

### Preferred meaning
The ways in which texts are encoded to encourage a fixed reading of the meaning(s) and ideologies contained within them.

### Realist aesthetic
A style of media production that deliberately which creates an illusion of realism (rather than drawing attention to the processes of production).

### Spectator
Often used interchangeably with the term 'audience'. In film theory, it also refers to the notion of the theoretical spectator who is constructed and addressed by the text – which may or may not be the same as the actual person consuming the text.

### Voyeurism
The act of viewing individuals without their knowledge. When watching a film, the spectator becomes a voyeur – watching the event that unfolds. The process of voyeurism is tied to visual pleasure.

# Filmography

| | | |
|---|---|---|
| *24 Hour Party People* | 2002 | Michael Winterbottom |
| *28 Days Later* | 2002 | Danny Boyle |
| *Age of Innocence, The* | 1993 | Martin Scorsese |
| *Alien* | 1979 | Ridley Scott |
| *Aliens* | 1986 | James Cameron |
| *Alien 3* | 1992 | David Fincher |
| *Alien Resurrection* | 1997 | Jean-Pierre Jeunet |
| *Ally McBeal* (TV Series) | 1997–2002 | Fox |
| *Austin Powers* | 1997 | Jay Roach |
| *Blue Steel* | 1990 | Kathryn Bigelow |
| *Bounce* | 2000 | Don Roos |
| *Captain Corelli's Mandolin* | 2001 | John Madden |
| *Carrington* | 1995 | Christopher Hamilton |
| *Chariots of Fire* | 1981 | Hugh Hudson |
| *Charlie's Angels* | 2000 | McG (sometimes credited as Joseph McGinty Nichol) |
| *Charlie's Angels: Full Throttle* | 2003 | McG (sometimes credited as Joseph McGinty Nichol) |
| *Chocolat* | 2000 | Lasse Halström |
| *Die Another Day* | 2002 | Lee Tamohori |
| *Elizabeth* | 1998 | Shekhar Kapur |
| *Emma* | 1996 | Douglas McGrath |
| *Friends* (TV series) | 1994–2004 | Warner Bros |
| *Fifth Element* | 1997 | Luc Besson |
| *Gangs of New York* | 2002 | Martin Scorsese |
| *High Fidelity* | 2000 | Stephen Frears |
| *Howards End* | 1992 | James Ivory |
| *K19: The Widowmaker* | 2002 | Kathryn Bigelow |

| | | |
|---|---|---|
| Life and Times of Rosie the Riveter, The | 1980 | Connie Fields |
| Maurice | 1987 | James Ivory |
| Moulin Rouge! | 2001 | Baz Luhrmann |
| Matrix,The | 1999 | Andy Wachowski, Larry Wachowski |
| Matrix: Reloaded, The | 2003 | Andy Wachowski, Larry Wachowski |
| Orlando | 1992 | Sally Potter |
| Passage to India, A | 1984 | David Lean |
| Perfect Murder, A | 1998 | Andrew Davis |
| Piano, The | 1993 | Jane Campion |
| Plunkett and Macleane | 1999 | Jake Scott |
| Point Break | 1991 | Kathryn Bigelow |
| Room With A View, A | 1986 | James Ivory |
| Royal Tenenbaums, The | 2001 | Wes Anderson |
| Sense and Sensibility | 1995 | Ang Lee |
| Sex and the City (TV series) | 1998–2004 | HBO |
| Shadowlands | 1993 | Richard Attenborough |
| Shakespeare in Love | 1998 | John Madden |
| Shallow Hal | 2001 | Bobby Farrelly, Peter Farrelly |
| Sliding Doors | 1998 | Peter Howitt |
| Spy Game | 2001 | Tony Scott |
| Strange Days | 1995 | Kathryn Bigelow |
| Talented Mr Ripley, The | 1999 | Anthony Minghella |
| Terminator, The | 1984 | James Cameron |
| Terminator 2: Judgement Day | 1991 | James Cameron |
| Thriller | 1979 | Sally Potter |
| Titanic | 1997 | James Cameron |
| Tom and Viv | 1994 | Brian Gilbert |
| Wedding Singer, The | 1998 | Frank Coraci |
| William Shakespeare's Romeo and Juliet | 1996 | Baz Luhrmann |
| Where Angels Fear to Tread | 1991 | Charles Sturridge |

# References and selected bibliography

R Angell (2002), *Getting into Films and Television: How to Spot the Opportunities and Find the Best Ways in*, How to Books.

V Bullough and B Bullough (1993), *Cross Dressing, Sex and Gender*, University of Pennsylvania Press

D Boyle (2002), Q & A session with Danny Boyle and Alex Garland following a special preview screening of *28 Days Later*, Tyneside Cinema, Newcastle-upon-Tyne, 22 October

S Bradley (2001), 'Cinematographers: The Ones Who Make the Beautiful Pictures', *The Silhouette*, at http://www.msu.mcmaster.ca/sil/archives/010208/arts/director.htm

S Bruzzi (1997), *Undressing Cinema: Costume and Identity in the Movies*. Routledge

P Church Gibson (1998), 'Film Costume', in P Church Gibson and J Hill (eds), *The Oxford Guide to Film Studies*, Oxford University Press

P Church Gibson (2000), 'Fewer Weddings and More Funerals: Changes in the Heritage Film', in R Murphy (ed), *British Cinema of the 90s*, bfi

M Citron (1990), 'Women's Film Production: Going Mainstream', in D Pribram, *Female Spectators: Looking at Film and Television*, Verso

P Cook (1996), *Fashioning the Nation: Costume and Identity in British Cinema*, bfi

C Craig (1991), 'Rooms without a View', *Sight and Sound*, June

J Cussons (2003), Telephone conversation with the author, 9 April

R Dyer (1994), 'Feeling English', *Sight and Sound*, March

R Dyer (1999), *Stars*, rev edn, bfi

R Dyer (2000), 'Nice Young Men Who Sell Antiques: Gay Men in Heritage Cinema', in G Vincendeau (ed), *Film/Literature/Heritage: A Sight and Sound Reader*, bfi

Freshminds Ltd (2003), *Employment in Film and Television in the UK. A Report on the Position of Women within the Industry.* Prepared for Women in Film and Television, March 2003.

T Gates (1995), *How to Get into the Film and TV Business*, Alma House

S Gilligan (2000), 'Gwyneth Paltrow', in S Bruzzi and P Church Gibson, *Fashion Cultures: Theories, Explorations and Analysis*, Routledge

M Goldberg (2002), 'Where Are the Female Directors?' at http://www.salon.com/ent/movies/feature/2002/08/27/women_directors

S Harper (1987), 'Historical Pleasures: Gainsborough Costume Melodrama', in C Gledhill (ed), *Home Is Where the Heart Is: Studies in Melodrama and the Woman's Film*, bfi

S Harper (1994), *Picturing the Past: The Rise and Fall of the British Costume Film*, bfi

S Hayward (1996), *Key Concepts in Cinema Studies*, Routledge

A Higson (1993), 'Re-presenting the National Past: Nostalgia and Pastiche in the Heritage Film', in L Friedman (ed), *British Cinema and Thatcherism: Fires Were Started*, UCL Press

A Higson (1996), The Heritage Film and British Cinema', in A Higson (ed), *Dissolving Views: Key Writings on British Cinema*, Cassell

J Hill (1999), 'The Heritage Film: Issues and Debates', in J Hill, *British Cinema: Issues and Themes*, bfi

A Holdsworth (1988), *Out of the Doll's House: The Story of Women in the Twentieth Century.* BBC Books.

A Hultkrans (1995) 'Reality Bytes. Interview with Hollywood director Kathryn Bigelow', in *Artforum International.* November 1995, Vol 34, no 3

P Hutchings (1995), 'A Disconnected View: Forster, Modernity and Film', in J Tambling (ed), *EM Forster*, Macmillan

I Katz (1996), 'Hollywood's Smash Its' *Guardian*, G2, 14 August

MM Lauzen (2001), 'Executive Summary', *The Celluloid Ceiling: Behind-the-Scenes. Employment of Women in the Top 250 Films of 2001* at www.moviesbywomen.com/stats2001.html

M M Lauzen (2002) 'Executive Summary', *Boxed in: Women on Screen and Behind the scenes in the 2001-2002 Prime-time Season*' at www.moviesbywomen.com/stats2002.html.

M M Lauzen (2003), 'Executive Summary', *The Celluloid Study* at www.moviesbywomen.com/stats2003.html

C McArthur (1981), 'Historical Drama', in T Bennett et al (eds), *Popular Television and Film*, Open University Press

C Monk (1994), *Sex, Politics and the Past: Merchant Ivory, the Heritage Film and Its Critics in 1980s and 1990s Britain*, MA dissertation, BFI/Birkbeck College

C Monk (1995), 'Sexuality and the Heritage', *Sight and Sound*, vol 5 no 10. Reprinted in G Vincendeau (ed) (2001), *Film/Literature/Heritage: A Sight and Sound Reader*, bfi

C Monk (1995), 'The British Heritage Film and Its Critics', *Critical Survey*, vol 7 no 2, pp116–24

C Monk (1996), 'The Heritage Film and Gendered Spectatorship', *Close Up: The Electronic Journal of British Cinema*, Issue 1, Winter. Article in two parts at http://www.shu.ac.uk/services/lc/closeup/monk.htm http://www.shu.ac.uk/services/lc/closeup/monk2.htm

C Monk (2001), British Film Institute Media Studies Conference. Unpublished conference session on heritage cinema

D Morgan (1997) 'Thelma Schoonmaker: Film Editor', In *Wide Angle/Closeup*. Available online at: http://members.aol.com/morgands1/closeup/text/cfthelm2.htm

T O'Regan (1995), 'Beyond "Australian film": Australian Cinema in the 1990s', in *Culture and Communication Reading Room: Writings on Australian Film* at http://wwwmcc.murdoch.edu.au/ReadingRoom/film/1990s.html

B Quart (1989), *Women Directors: The Emergence of a New Cinema*, Praeger

B Quart (1994), '*The Piano* – Review', *Cineaste*, vol 20 no 3

H Rubenstein (1999), 'Gwyneth When She Glitters', *In Style* magazine, January, at http://www.gwynethpaltrow.org

M Shnayerson (2000), 'Today Belongs to Gwyneth', *Vanity Fair*

Skillset, *A–Z of Jobs in the Audio Visual Industries* at http://www.skillset.org/careers/home.asp

J Stacey (1994), *Stargazing: Hollywood Cinema and Female Spectatorship*, Routledge

S Street (2001), *Costume and Cinema: Dress Codes in Popular Culture*, Wallflower Press

Y Tasker (1993), *Spectacular Bodies: Gender, Genre and Action Cinema*, Routledge

Y Tasker (1998), *Working Girls: Gender and Sexuality in Popular Cinema*, Routledge

Y Tasker (1999), 'Bigger than Life', reprinted in Jose Arroyo (ed.) (2000), *Action/Spectacle Cinema: A Sight and Sound Reader*, bfi

S Thornham (1997), *Passionate Detachments: An Introduction to Feminist Film Theory*, Arnold

S Thornham (1999), *Feminist Film Theory: A Reader*, Edinburgh University Press

D Waters (2002), 'Women Directors Fight Back', BBC News, at http://news.bbc.co.uk/1/hi/entertainment/film/2420713

R White (1999), 'Psychoanalysis', in P Cook and M Bernik, *The Cinema Book*, 2nd edn, bfi

T Wollen (1991), 'Over Our Shoulders: Nostalgic Screen Fictions for the 1980s', in Harvey and Corner (eds), *Enterprise and Heritage*, Routledge

# Websites

http://www.imdb.co.uk – Internet Movie Database website, an excellent starting point for searching for films, cast and crew

http://www.filmunlimited.co.uk – The Guardian's film pages

http://www.bbc.co.uk – the BBC website

http://www.oscars.com – official Oscar website which includes details of all previous winners

http://www.wftv.org.uk – Women in Film and Television (professional association)

http://www.widc.org – Women in the Director's Chair website

http://www.moviesbywomen.com – Movies by Women website

http://www.cinenova.org – Distributors of women's films

http://www.wmm.com – Women Make Movies website

http://www.kathrynbigelow.com/index.html – Extensive fan site on Kathryn Bigelow

http://www.gwynethpaltrow.org – Extensive fan site on Gwyneth Paltrow, including lots of images

http://www.bfi.org.uk/gateway/categories/womeninfilmandtv/ – bfi's Gateway for Women in Film and TV

http://www.bfi.org.uk/nationallibrary/collections/bibliographies/women_film.pdf – selection of material covering the subject of women and film, all held by the British Film Institute

# Acknowledgements

There are many people to whom thanks are due for their ongoing help and encouragement both during the production of this guide and while I juggle a full-time teaching post in FE, PhD research and 'Life'.

I would like to thank my editor, Vivienne Clark, for her help, guidance, patience and encouragement throughout its production; Stella Bruzzi, for her guidance, feedback and support with my PhD research, parts of which inform this guide; my students at Hartlepool College of Further Education (especially my A2 Media groups during the period 2001–3), with whom I have worked through many of the ideas in this guide and shared my 'obsession' with textual analysis and costume.

Thanks also to my friends and colleagues for their various kinds and degrees of support, especially (but by no means only) Nicola Beckett and Joanne Potts.

Extra special thanks must go, though, to Steve, my parents and my brother for their love, support and encouragement, and for listening (and at least pretending) to be interested.

This guide is dedicated in loving memory to my Gran-ma.